ALLEN RIDER GUIDES

RIDING CROSS-COUNTRY

ALLEN RIDER GUIDES

Riding Cross-Country

Martin Diggle

J. A. Allen

London

British Library Cataloguing in Publication Data

Diggle, Martin
Riding cross-country.—(Allen rider guides)
1. Cross-country (Horsemanship)
I. Title
798.2'3   SF295.6

ISBN 0–85131–426–0

Published in Great Britain by
J. A. Allen & Company Limited,
1, Lower Grosvenor Place, Buckingham Palace Road,
London, SW1W 0EL

© Martin Diggle, 1986
2nd edition printed 1990

Text illustrations Maggie Raynor
Text design Nancy Lawrence

Printed in Hong Kong by Dah Hua Printing Co. Ltd.
Typeset by Setrite Typesetters Ltd.

Acknowledgements

The author would like to acknowledge with thanks the assistance given by the following organisations and individuals in the writing of this book:

The British Horse Society for approval of the author's interpretation of *Rules for Official Horse Trials*. Members of the Arab Horse Society for information regarding the current state of Ride and Tie events. Mrs Rosemary Slater for a most informative conversation concerning the organisation of obstacle rides. Joyce Bellamy for helpful comments during the draft.

Contents

— Contents —

List of Illustrations

Preface

Some years ago, when I was taking my first steps towards competitive cross-country riding, my rather formidable, but very helpful, teacher told me: 'There are two ways you can succeed: you can get experience on all sorts of horses, and learn to ride them effectively, or you can get rich and buy a good horse. However, if you just buy success, it will only last as long as it takes to ruin the horse.' She added: 'My horses are nothing special, but you can learn a lot from them if you're prepared to try.'

I recommend this philosophy to all readers.

Introduction

This book has been written to pursue further some of the ideas touched upon in *Riding Over Jumps*, which is an initial guide to jumping in general. Behind *Riding Cross-Country* lies the observation that, once riders have learnt the rudiments of flatwork and jumping, they tend to start thinking seriously about the various branches of equestrian sport, and how these may be explored. Since a number of equestrian sports have a common basis in cross-country riding, it follows that someone who can negotiate varied terrain and obstacles safely and effectively, perhaps on a strange horse, has a lot of possibilities and pleasures open to him.

I hope, therefore, that this book will not only be of interest and assistance from a technical aspect, but that it may also help readers to broaden their horizons. As with *Riding Over Jumps*, this book is aimed chiefly at the adult rider of limited experience, whose main asset is keenness, and who may well be short of time and money! Within this framework I have endeavoured to consider the requirements of three main groups of readers: those who are taking their very first steps in cross-country riding, those who might be termed 'average' club riders, and who have participated in the odd club hunter trial, and those rather more experienced riders who may be sharing a horse, or who are permitted by a commercial establishment to take a horse to local shows.

Although at certain points in the text the horse is referred to almost as though it were owned by the reader, I am, in fact, assuming that sole ownership would be the exception rather than the rule. I do, however, feel that anyone who rides cross-country should treat the horse as if it were their own, and that learning to pay attention to the horse's welfare, tack, etc. can only prove beneficial to the rider as well as the horse.

1
Defining Riding Cross-Country

If one asks 'What is riding cross-country?', the basic answer is 'Crossing the countryside on horseback.' When this statement is examined more closely, however, it becomes apparent that it may encompass many permutations of circumstance. Terrain and obstacles (whether natural, or the product of the course builder) may be of almost infinite variety, ground conditions ('going') can vary greatly, there are the rules or customs of the relevant sport to be observed, and many other factors including rider's knowledge (or otherwise) of the terrain, rider's aspirations (trying to win/ enjoying a day out), and, of course, the horse.

From this colourful and varied background, a number of sports have emerged and evolved, the main ones being:

Hunting . . . .
Individual Hunter Trials . . . .
Pair and Team Hunter Trials   Team Chasing
'Mock Hunting'   Drag Hunting
        Hunt 'Rides'
        'Old Style' Point-to-Points

Cross-country phase of Eventing
  (One Day) . . . . (Two and Three Day)
Ride and Tie
Obstacle Rides

        Long Distance Riding

These sports are listed in two columns in order to differentiate on a broad basis between those within the compass of the 'ordinary' rider (left column), and those which require considerable experience, a talented horse and, perhaps, special skills (right column). Where two sports are listed opposite each other, this indicates that they are broadly equivalent or, at least, have a good deal in common. The dotted lines indicate a sport especially capable of accommodating a wide spectrum of experience on the part of both horse and rider.

In practice of course, the delineations are much less straightforward than they appear in print. Many levels are involved and the rider's enjoyment of, and success in, all the activities will be enhanced as experience and ability increase. With regard to the 'advanced' sports, in fact, success (or even participation) in them will be dependent upon the rider having served a thorough apprenticeship at a less exalted level and, since this book is chiefly about learning the basics, it will not deal specifically with these activities.

That is not to suggest, however, that the reader may not one day be capable of performing at such levels, so here, briefly we shall look at what they involve.

Team Chasing

Originally the brainchild of Douglas Bunn, who held inaugural events at Hickstead in the early 1970s. Teams, usually of four riders, have to negotiate a cross-country course as quickly as possible, with the time of the third rider home normally counting for the team. Falls and refusals are unpenalised, except insofar as they add to time.

This has become a highly-competitive sport, with very experienced riders on high-class horses competing over formidable courses. There are 'novice' classes at some events, but the term tends to be relative. For those who like the idea of team competitions, some hunter trials hold 'pairs' or 'teams of three' classes. These usually take place round a more genuine 'novice' course, and will be discussed later in the book.

Drag Hunting

This involves hounds following a pre-laid artificial scent. Although it seems to have originated from instances of certain old time Masters of Hounds 'cheating' in order to ensure a good run, it is no longer looked upon as a substitute for foxhunting, and drag hunts exist as completely separate entities.

The main purpose of a drag hunt is to organise fast rides over well-fenced country. Many are to be found in parts where the countryside has been subject to urban encroachment, one advantage of the drag being that it can be laid along suitable lines within a relatively confined area.

Drag hunting has a certain tradition of dare-devil, with participants tending to be mounted on ex-steeplechasers and event horses, and many obstacles being pretty formidable. Apart from the necessity of being well-mounted, riding skill and experience are pre-requisites, and some drag hunts have links with cross-country clubs, and make a point of encouraging the development of good riding.

One hunt with such links is the Coakham Bloodhounds in Kent. Bloodhound packs are not, strictly speaking, drag hunts, since the hounds do not follow an artificial scent, but a human one. The human in question is usually a local cross-country athlete, putting in some training whilst assisting friends involved with the hunt. He is in no danger of being devoured if caught, although he may find himself getting severely licked. This form of the sport tends to produce rather slower 'runs' than the scorching pace of hounds on a strong artificial scent, but although it may give riders a little more time in which to catch loose horses, it is still hardly sedate.

Hunt 'Rides'

These are not really a recognised sport as such, but rather impromptu races across country. They are organised by various hunts, usually on an annual basis, for their own members, and perhaps those of adjacent hunts. Although there is no obligation for participants to race, there are prizes for the first home in various categories (first farmer, first heavyweight, etc.). These events are, in spirit, quite close to the original point-to-points, and an ability to cross country somewhat faster than discretion would dictate, in the midst of a number of other riders trying to do likewise, is a pre-requisite for success.

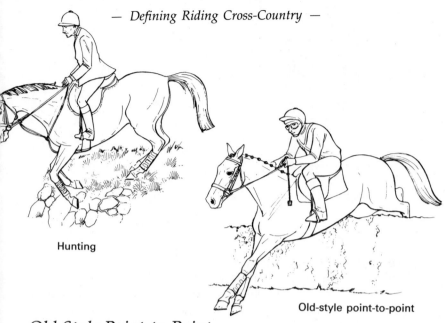

Hunting

Old-style point-to-point

Old Style Point-to-Point

As with hunt 'Rides', participation is normally restricted to members of the organising hunt. The event will be run as one of the races at a point-to-point meeting, and is subject to the main rules of racing, although entry qualifications for both horse and rider are less restrictive than for a normal point-to-point.

Old style point-to-points blend natural obstacles with 'regulation' fences, and fill a gap between hunt rides and formal amateur racing. They require considerable courage, skill and fitness on the part of the rider, and a horse which could be described, at least, as a 'good hunter'

Two and Three Day Events

These are organised, in Britain, by the Horse Trials Group of the British Horse Society, and are open only to horses which have achieved considerable success at official One Day level. The reader will doubtless be familiar with the variety, spectacle and demands of Badminton, Burghley, etc., and appreciate that this is strictly 'top of the tree' stuff.

Eventing   Long distance riding

Long Distance Riding

This sport, which perhaps receives less publicity than it merits, entails riding long distances within specified time limits. The distances are generally between 80 to 120 km (50 to 75 miles). The time limits are split into 'gold', 'silver' and 'bronze' categories, so that newcomers to the sport can work their way up to the 'gold' as their experience and knowledge of the demands of the sport increase.

The rides usually take place across demanding terrain (Exmoor being one popular venue), and there are stringent veterinary checks at intervals, with horses which fail being ineligible to continue. Participation requires ownership of a sound and hardy horse, personal fitness, a lot of available time and, most importantly, a very high standard of horsemastership.

The sport is, however, essentially cheaper than several others, and does not require an especially high standard of technical riding ability, and it is therefore popular amongst those who just enjoy riding, and who take a justifiable pride in keeping their horse as fit and well as he can be.

Those sports which may be considered accessible to any reasonably competent cross-country rider will be discussed in some detail at a later stage, but in the meantime let us examine the main aims of cross-country riding, and the means by which the rider can obtain the techniques and understanding necessary to achieve those aims.

2

Aims of the Cross-Country Rider

The basic aims, which can be considered common to all cross-country sports, are to cross varied terrain, whether unknown or along a pre-determined route, with regard to the following:
1) Safety of horse and rider.
2) As little exertion on the horse's (and rider's!) part as is compatible with circumstances.
3) Negotiating obstacles as required cleanly.
4) Avoiding interference with, or damage to, other horses and riders, and, in some cases, members of the public and landowners.
5) Adhering to the rules of the sport concerned.
For the benefit of the reader who is taking first steps in cross-country riding, let us consider the preliminary riding skills which are required as a basis for working toward these aims.

Preliminary Requirements of the Rider

FLATWORK The rider should have attained a level of riding on the flat where he has a reasonably good position, with some depth of seat, and is able to retain his balance, and an acceptable contact with the horse's mouth at walk, trot and canter. He should have some knowledge of the principle of sending the horse forward onto the bit, and be capable of obtaining some lengthening and shortening of stride on a well-school horse.

JUMPING The rider should have experience of jumping small knock-down fences, and be capable of negotiating a basic course of such fences. *It is very important* that he has established a safe and effective technique over this type of obstacle, and can follow the horse's movement without 'anticipating' the fence and becoming unbalanced forwards. The rider who frequently exhibits this fault *must* rectify it in the school before tackling solid cross country obstacles, in order to avoid a considerable risk of injury.

Effective technique also encompasses the supposition that the rider does not habitually exhibit other serious errors in negotiating straightforward fences. (These errors and their remedies are discussed in *Riding Over Jumps*.)

RIDING OUT It is very useful if the rider has preliminary experience of hacking out in open country. This, in itself, is a basic form of cross-country riding, and will give some grounding in controlling the horse at all gaits, sitting in balance up and down hill, and, hopefully, sitting still and allowing the horse extra rein if he should stumble over rough ground. A well-conducted riding holiday, especially in an upland area, can provide the more novice rider with considerable experience in this respect.

FITNESS The rider will perform better in all branches of equitation if he is reasonably fit, but this is especially true of cross-country, which can be quite physically demanding on a good horse, and downright exhausting on a difficult one. The rider who 'runs out of steam' part way round a course is not only of no assistance to his horse; he may well be an actual hinderance, and put the partnership at physical risk. By the same token, cross-country riding is not recommended for anyone suffering from an injury which affects (or which may be aggravated by) their riding, nor for anyone recovering from a weakening illness.

ATTITUDE Books on riding have a tendency to set great store by technique, and ignore the mental approach of the rider. Attitude can, however, have a great influence upon riding, just as it can upon other sports. I am thinking for the moment of the rider's approach to coping with his own circumstances, rather than his attitude to fellow riders as, for instance, embodied in the etiquette of the hunting field.

It has been said that the most important characteristics of the cross-country horse are boldness and cleverness, and this applies equally to the rider. With the horse, cleverness usually means an ability to get out of trouble (find a fifth leg, as the saying is), whereas with the rider, it should refer to the intelligence and ability to avoid trouble: we shall examine some thoughts along those lines in due course. Boldness is not to be confused with recklessness. If it were the same thing, it could hardly go hand in glove with cleverness. It is probably better described by the phrase 'being positive', and this is the key to successful cross-country riding.

Being positive is an attitude which can be adopted by the most inexperienced cross-country rider. Whereas his awareness of his inexperience may create a diffidence somewhat at odds with 'boldness', he can nevertheless try his best to ride the horse forward, maintain control and approach obstacles in a decisive fashion. Such initial determination and decisiveness form an important foundation upon which the rider can build as confidence and experience increase. Furthermore, in addition to helping the rider to perform better, they seem to be influences which 'get through' to the horse mentally, increasing his confidence in the rider.

Conversely, indecision, lack of determination, or worst of all, a lackadaisical approach can quickly sap a horse's confidence, or encourage him to take matters into his own hands. Both states of affairs are most undesirable in any branch of riding, but especially so in the circumstances of riding across country.

To sum up then, the cross-country rider must be prepared from the beginning to adopt a wholehearted attitude, and to cultivate the ability to make firm decisions and relay his intentions clearly to the horse.

Outdoor Control

The rider who measures up to the requirements outlined above can be considered to have reached a stage at which it is reasonable to begin tackling solid fences in the open, suitably mounted and under competent instruction. Before going on to discuss ideas and techniques, however, I would like to deal with a more fundamental and very real problem which confronts many riders these days, and that is the transition from 'indoor' to 'outdoor' riding.

I have said that one of the prerequisites for the novice cross-country rider is some experience of riding in the open, but I know that in many cases the initial opportunity to begin riding cross-country will occur before the rider has really had sufficient outdoor experience. A lot of people nowadays begin to ride in, and spend virtually all their formative time in, an indoor school or enclosed arena. Whilst this is highly desirable in early stages from a safety aspect, it can eventually give the rider a false perspective of riding in general, and his abilities in particular. Experienced riders will know that most horses undergo some degree of character transformation when released from the confines of the school into the wide open spaces, generally showing more enthusiasm and sparkle, and perhaps getting a bit excited and 'cheeky'. However, the rider who experiences this for the first time is likely to suffer a jolt to his confidence when he finds that the horse he has been riding quite competently in the school suddenly pays scant attention to his aids, and starts to generate more 'free forward movement' than the rider knows how to contain.

I have witnessed this on many occasions, and heard rather startled riders declaring that their horse has 'gone loony', 'pulled like a train', etc. In a reputable stable none of these colourful descriptions should be true, and in the vast majority of cases they are not, but they do relay the 'culture shock' experienced by the riders, and this has to be resolved in order to avoid a damaging effect upon their confidence as cross-country exponents.

It will help the rider about to make the transition to riding in the open if he can come to terms with the requirements of the cross-country horse in theory, before experiencing any practical problems. To perform well across country, and give a good ride, a horse must be at least reasonably fit, fairly free-going, and have a basic enthusiasm for the job. The reason for fitness is self-evident; the desirability of a free-going, enthusiastic horse will become evident to anyone who has to ride a sluggish or nappy mount round even a short cross-country course – it is very hard work, and jumping solid obstacles on a horse which needs riding flat out to even approach them is not much fun. A certain degree of 'bounce' and exuberance are, therefore to be sought after and welcomed in the cross-country horse. The novice rider will, however, welcome them much more when he knows how to control them, so let us look at the adjustments he must make in order to do so:

Firstly, the rider coming out of the school should make the simple adjustment of shortening his stirrup leathers a couple of holes. Apart from the assumption that cross-country riding is likely to involve some jumping, the shorter leathers serve other purposes:

1) At the faster gaits, the cross-country rider will usually want to be in a poised position just out of the saddle, and this is facilitated by shorter leathers.

2) Riding over uneven ground, it is quite easy to lose a stirrup if riding 'school' length. Apart from the basic inconvenience this causes, if the rider is having control problems, these will not be made easier by riding with only one stirrup.

3) Across country, the rider will tend to rely more upon the stirrups to assist position and balance than he would in the school. This is not to say that natural balance is less important across country (in fact, it is essential), but merely reflects the nature and practicalities of the sport. Given these circumstances, any tendency to be 'reaching' for the stirrups is to be avoided.

4) Shorter stirrups actually facilitate control of a 'strong' horse. We shall study this point in more detail later.

Secondly, the rider will probably have to make some adjustment to his approach to the horse, and the application of the aids. The degree of adjustment will depend upon the horse being ridden, and the prevailing circumstances, but in any instance where a horse is proving 'keen' or 'fresh' it is important for the rider to realise that it will require *more* direction than usual from the saddle, and must be ridden *forward*. The rider should be sure, above all else, to keep his legs 'on' the horse, and ride it forward onto the rein contact.

In order to do so, and in order to obtain other basic responses, he may find that he needs to be firmer with the horse than past experience would suggest is necessary. This does not imply that the aids should be harsh, nor that they should depart from accepted equestrian principles (leg before hand, whip and leg together, etc.). They should, however, be strong enough for the horse to respect them from the start. Here, the rider can draw upon his 'school' experience; he will have learnt that, although the principle is to apply the aids as lightly as is effective, this can, in some circumstances, mean 'quite strongly'. The term 'aid', after all, implies 'active assistance' – not some diffident suggestion which is easily ignored. To illustrate this point, I recall the occasion when I heard a rider say: 'I gave the right aids, but the horse didn't halt.' The flaw in this logic is that the *right* aids in the circumstances would have been those which *did* elicit the halt. The lesson to be learnt with regard to riding cross-country is that, while the rider can usually 'have another go' in a flatwork session, he must always be seeking prompt and correct responses to his initial commands when outdoors. This becomes especially apparent when one considers safety aspects (particularly those involving third parties), and the high penalties incurred in cross-country competitions for even a single refusal.

Rider Errors When Seeking Control

Whilst every effort should be made to adhere to the principles outlined above, it must be admitted that it is one thing to read about the theory, and quite another to put it into practice at the first attempt. Most riders will, in fact, make initial errors, and since these often stem from doing what seems logical or correct in the heat of the moment, it is worth examining the common mistakes in order to see why the rider should try to avoid them.

FIGHTING THE HORSE   It is important that the rider thinks in terms of controlling, rather than subduing, the horse. Taking a fierce grip on the reins and trying to wrestle him into submission will only create confusion and resentment on the horse's part, making him nappy or causing him to throw his head up and go hollow-backed. The hollow-backed outline is particularly undesirable since, not only does it make the horse harder to control, it also renders it physically impossible for him to move correctly at any gait or jump in good style.

UNDER-RIDING   We have discussed the possibility of the rider new to cross-country discovering that his 'standard' aids may not always be sufficient in the new environment, but that is not really the same thing as under-riding, by which I mean adopting a deliberate policy of only giving very light aids. This is sometimes seen in riders who have developed quite good technique and position in the school, and think that they can use their ability to sit still and ride quietly in order to put an excited horse 'to sleep'.

Although the principle of quiet aids is a good one, in practice subtlety and tact often have to be blended with considerable firmness, or else the horse may quickly realise that he is being humoured rather than ridden. One of the main drawbacks of over-reliance upon the 'quiet' approach is, in fact, that it may have some effect for a while and then fail suddenly, either for the reason above or because the horse becomes startled, or is turned towards home or another object of magnetic interest. If this failure occurs, and the rider has no other ideas to resort to, his confidence may be quite badly dented. One of the most disconcerting moments in equitation is when a rider's belief in a 'secret' is shattered, and the situation is worsened if this revelation coincides with his being 'carted'.

The other drawbacks of under-riding are firstly that the horse may just ignore the rider from the beginning, and secondly that, if the rider's intentions are fulfilled, he may well find that the horse is 'switched off' to the extent that he is no longer concentrating on the job in hand, and is moving with too little impulsion, both serious faults in the cross-country horse.

TAKING RIDER'S LEGS 'OFF' THE HORSE   This very serious error is a reversion to the beginner's misconception that 'reins mean stop and legs mean go'. Whilst it is understandable that a flustered novice rider could react this way in the heat of the moment, hoping that it might cause the horse to slow down, the action will, in fact, just surrender control to the horse. I have, nonetheless, witnessed incidents of bystanders advising riders in difficulty to 'take your legs off'. Such advice is dangerous nonsense, and should be ignored. I do not suggest that the rider on a keen, sensitive horse should wrap himself round it like a hungry anaconda, but his legs should be in sufficient contact for the horse to be aware of them.

INACTION   It is not unknown for the more phlegmatic or intrepid rider who finds himself more or less out of control to just sit there and enjoy the experience. Although this level of fatalism can, in some respects, be admired, it is not an attitude conducive to negotiating the countryside successfully, and it may endanger not only the rider himself, but others also. A slightly less extreme version of this attitude can be seen in the rider who assumes that, because his mount is happy to career around as the mood takes him, he will also look after himself and the rider, and automatically jump anything in his path. Such thinking is bound to end in disillusionment, and should be abandoned before it also results in disaster.

Equine 'Centres' and the Rider's Posture _____

Having looked initially at general control of the horse in the open, we should now consider further the postural alterations which the rider will have to make in order to restrain or assist his horse according to the various demands of crossing country at speed. The purpose of altering the posture is to directly influence the horse's locomotion, and the keys to this locomotion are the two 'centres' in the horse's body. These 'centres' are the centre of gravity and the centre of motion.

The centre of gravity is rather nomadic. With the horse standing correctly at rest, it will be located vertically beneath his spine, at a point just a few centimetres in front of the rider's knee. As the horse accelerates, however, the centre of gravity will move forward up to a certain point, and its precise location will alter almost continually throughout the cycle of the horse's stride.

The centre of motion is rather more static, and could be crudely described as the midway point between the hind and fore limbs. It is located along the line of the horse's spine roughly beneath the rider's coccyx (spinal tail), assuming that the rider is sitting normally on a well-made saddle. It is this juxtaposition of the base of the rider's spine and the horse's centre of motion which is so crucial when schooling a horse on the flat, and in dressage generally, since it gives the rider the wherewithal to use his seat and back either to give forward driving aids or to 'hold' (restrain) the horse. Since the correct principles of equitation apply to all its branches, this relationship between rider's position and the centre of motion is important to the cross-country rider, although he may not use the seat and back in quite the same way as would be appropriate to the dressage arena, adapting, instead, to the different circumstances. If, then, the rider wishes to allow his horse to move forward as freely and easily as possible, he should alter his own posture so that the burden of his weight is over the horse's centre of gravity. If he wishes either to drive the horse forwards, or to restrain it, he will need to position himself over (or, in the case of strong restraint, slightly behind) the centre of motion.

In cross-country riding, the 'classic' gait is a swinging canter, with the horse moving at a 'cruising speed' which he can maintain for a considerable length of time without tiring. When moving in this manner, the horse should be going forward into the rider's hands, not fighting for his head, but ready and willing to quicken if asked. Once settled into his rhythm, he should not require 'reminder' aids, but should just bowl along until asked to change speed or gait. Although the rider should be mentally alert, monitoring the 'feel' he is getting from the horse, and thinking ahead, he should need to make very little physical contribution to the partnership, other than to keep in balance with the horse.

In such circumstances, the rider should adopt a poised posture. This is attained by folding the upper body forward from the hips, and allowing the backside to come far enough out of the saddle to avoid bumping in time to the canter motion. The rider's legs should remain on the girth, with flexion of knees and ankles maintained, and any tendency to 'get out of the saddle' by straightening the legs should be avoided.

With the horse moving freely forward, this posture will be readily maintained by a combination of balance and a light grip with the thighs. There should be no need for the rider to lean on the horse's wither, and any tendency to do so suggests that the rider *has* straightened his legs, or has allowed the lower leg to move back behind the girth.

The angle of inclination of the upper body should be

determined by the speed of the horse, since the purpose of the postural adjustment is to move the rider's weight closer to the horse's centre of gravity, and we have seen that this will tend to be located further forward as speed increases. The rider should be sure that the posture adopted is in accord with the 'feel' of the horse's movement, and is not merely an artificial pose which he hopes will look good. It should be noted that no useful purpose can be served by getting 'in front' of the centre of gravity; such a position is of no assistance to the horse, and is most precarious for the rider.

Should it become necessary to actively restrain the horse (as opposed to merely asking him to slow down, or do a downward transition), the rider can readily adapt his posture from the poised position. Instead of the upper body being inclined forward, it is brought back virtually to the vertical, so that the burden of the rider's weight is over the centre of motion. The rider's back should be straight and, if the horse is very 'strong', it will be helpful if the seat remains just out of the saddle initially, so that he can bring his weight, as well as the strength of the big back and legs muscles to bear. The lower legs may be braced forward a little in front of the girth in circumstances where restraint, though necessary, may affect the horse's balance to some extent, but they should not be rammed out like cart shafts, since this will effectively take them 'off' the horse, and encourage the upper body to pivot back uselessly behind the vertical. From this restraining posture, the rider should maintain a steady contact with one rein and check and release firmly with the other, repeating the motion until the horse begins to respond. (If more than a few 'check and release' motions are needed, the rider should periodically reverse the rein aids.) Once the horse does start to show signs of steadying the rider can move his weight forward a little, and return his seat to the saddle, so that he is in a position to ride the horse forward under full control for a few strides before, if desired, he once again sends him into his 'cruising' gait and speed. The rider should also revert from the poised position to a 'normal' seated posture on any other occasion when he needs to actively influence the horse's movement, for instance: if he senses any incipient disobedience – shying, napping or bucking; when he wishes to change gait;

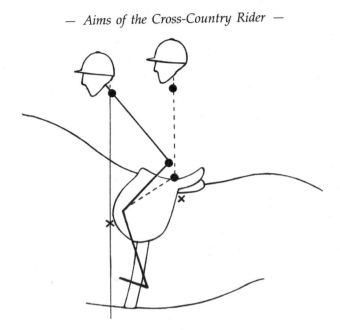

Diagram to illustrate examples of poised position (solid line) and restraining posture (broken line)

whenever riding an approach to a jump.

With regard to the last circumstance, I have explained in some detail in *Riding Over Jumps* why the last few strides of approach should be ridden with the rider seated in the saddle. In the context of 'centres', we have established that it is when the rider is above the centre of motion that he is best positioned to control the horse, and control is what is required on the approach. The rider who assumes that his poised position will, of itself, get the partnership safely over the jump may get away with it for a short while given a bold horse and straightforward obstacles, but he will be quickly dissuaded from his opinion when confronted with a more difficult horse or fence.

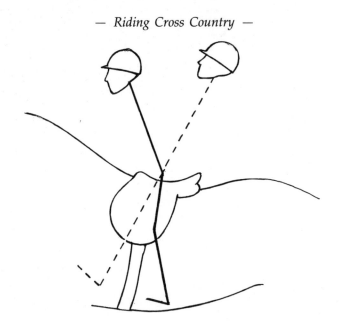

Diagram to illustrate incorrect postures. Solid figure shows incorrect attempt at poised position. Rider is tipping forward onto fork, with whole of leg too far back. A weak and precarious position from which it would be difficult to revert to correct restraining posture. Broken line shows a misconceived attempt at restraint. The leg is too far forward – effectively 'off' the horse. Rider sitting on back of saddle with upper body merely leaning backward. In this position, the rider is unable to do anything but take a 'dead' pull on the reins. A classic posture of the hopelessly 'carted'

Hills and Slopes

Riding up, down and across slopes must be an integral part of the cross-country rider's art; indeed, in some areas he will be doing little else. Since the horse originated as a species of the plains, he is not primarily designed for feats of mountaineering, although some breeds and types can adapt surprisingly well. Most horses can, in fact, negotiate pretty steep slopes if correctly ridden, and this entails the rider having a sympathetic understanding of the physical and mechanical demands being made upon his mount.

RIDING UPHILL   Given suitable going, and a degree of steepness appropriate to the gait, the horse can move uphill effectively in any gait, although the incline will cause his stride length to be relatively shorter than it would be on the flat.

Although travelling uphill obviously demands increased expenditure of energy on the horse's part, it is mechanically easier for him than moving down, or across, a slope. The reason for this is that his source of locomotive power is in the hind limbs and quarters, and is therefore well positioned for the task of pushing his own, and the rider's, weight up the hill. A parallel to this would be a person wishing to manoeuvre a loaded wheelbarrow up a slope. The easiest method is to get the body weight well behind the barrow, and drive it forward with the power of the legs, the task being further simplified if the load in the barrow is stable.

The rider's role then, in assisting the horse, is to ensure that his hind quarters are unencumbered, and that the horse's 'load' is as stable and compact as possible. Both aims are achieved by the rider getting his weight as close as possible to the horse's centre of gravity and keeping it there, and the method of doing so is, as with jumping, to fold forward from the hips.

The degree of folding necessary will be determined by the steepness of the incline, but any rider with a modicum of sensibility to the horse's movement will feel a natural desire to fold forward going up any significant slope, and will also feel when he is in harmony with his mount's movement. If the slope is particularly steep it will, in fact, be virtually impossible for the rider to fold too far forward, and he may end up with his chest almost touching the base of the horse's neck. In such circumstances, it is important that the principles of 'folding' are adhered to; that is that the back remains straight, the head remains up and looking forward, and the leg position is maintained. When moving uphill, the horse will usually carry his head and neck quite low, partly as a balancing process and partly because the activity of the hocks and quarters will tend to put him into a 'rounded' outline (hence the value of riding uphill as a schooling/ balancing process).

The rider should allow the horse to take any extra rein he requires (whilst maintaining a light contact), although his own position will be such that the overall rein length will not be very long. He should use his legs to produce sufficient impulsion for the horse to maintain his rhythm and purpose, but should not 'niggle' the horse into rushing.

Some horses naturally try to hurry up hills, just as some people automatically run up stairs. If the rider feels his horse wanting to hurry, he can usually dissuade him from doing so with quite a light restraining aid (keeping the leg on and resisting gently with

Riding uphill. Rider folding substantially from the hips. In order to avoid over-shortening the reins while in this posture, it may be expedient to angle the elbows in both planes more than usual. However, the hands should not be tucked into the stomach

the hand) without any need to alter the upper body posture. This light restraint, coupled with the prospect of extra expenditure of energy up the hill, will usually persuade the horse to take things steady. The full restraining posture previously described should not normally be necessary in these circumstances and should only be adopted uphill if the rider is literally being run away with, since, in these conditions, it can have a serious effect on the horse's balance.

RIDING DOWNHILL Going downhill in a measured and balanced fashion is not very easy for the horse, since he has to contend both with the effects of gravity and the fact that his rear end, the source of locomotive power, is higher up the slope than the rest of his body. This combination of circumstances means that if he does not make efforts to regulate his movement, he will proceed in an unbalanced and precipitate fashion. Furthermore, as anyone who has gone down a very steep slope on foot will know, loss of balance can alter short, controlled steps into a stumbling run very suddenly, and the process is extremely difficult to reverse.

Although, despite these difficulties, horses of suitable conformation and temperament can learn to cope with amazingly steep slopes, it is true to say that no horse can do so unless correctly ridden. While technique is of obvious importance in these circumstances, it must be complemented by a sense of 'feel' for the horse's motion and balance, and the rider should try to absorb some of this 'feel' whilst practising down short slopes on good going before attempting either to walk down steep hills or to negotiate gentler slopes at the faster gaits.

WALKING DOWN STEEP HILLS Although walk is the only gait at which a horse can be expected to negotiate really steep slopes, the lateral nature of the gait is not really in his favour, and most horses, other than the really well balanced, will tend to walk downhill with a rolling motion.

The reason for this is that, after taking a step with a hindleg, the walking horse must next move the foreleg on the same side of his body; the very leg which he has just braced in order to contain the downward thrust produced by the hindleg. In order to try and modify this rather stilted and mechanically difficult movement, the horse attempts to move both legs on the same side of his body as nearly as possible at the same time, thus abandoning the four-time rhythm of the true walk. Rather than a regular 1 . . 2 . . 3 . . 4 . . rhythm, there is a 1 . 2 swagger 3 . 4 effect.

It is important that the rider does all he can to minimise any loss of straightness on the horse's part since, if the quarters swing too far out of line, there is a real risk that the horse may lose his balance completely, and slide down the hill sideways or even fall. The rider should, therefore, encourage his mount to take short, steady steps, which will give him more time to balance himself and 'meter out' his own impulsion, thereby minimising loss of rhythm and the consequential crookedness.

The rider must be sitting in a position which is of assistance to the horse in terms of weight distribution and balance, and from which the aids can be applied in a subtle and non-disruptive manner. He must, therefore, be still and secure in the saddle, and ensure that he is not tilted to one side, which would certainly affect the horse's straightness. The legs should remain at the girth, gently encouraging the horse to maintain steady forward progress, and ready to correct tactfully any incipient crooked-ness. The rein contact should be light and 'confidential'. Whilst no attempt should be made to 'prop the horse up' with the reins, he will (especially if used to going 'on the bit') find the contact a valuable 'point of reference' from which to adjust his tempo. Furthermore, should he become a little flustered, and give the impression that he wants to hurry down the hill and get it over, a timely closing of the fingers round the reins, coupled with a soothing word, may be sufficient to re-establish his confidence and rhythm. This action, it should be stressed, has nothing in common with an attempt to tug the horse up with the reins in the event of his suffering a serious loss of balance, and scrambling down the slope in a desperate attempt to keep his feet. In such circumstances the only course of action open to the rider is to sit still, allow the horse to take all the rein he requires, and leave worrying about regaining control until the horse is able to regain his equilibrium. Any interference, especially with the horse's head, will be counter-productive at best, and probably disastrous.

Some horses naturally prefer to go downhill with their noses virtually on the ground, and, if this is the case, the rider should ignore his own concern at having 'nothing in front of him', and let the horse get on with it. (In truth, he will have little alternative, since he can only raise the horse's head either by strong use of the legs, which will probably make his mount hurry, or by pulling on the reins, which is just not on.) Regardless of the length of rein taken, however, the contact should be maintained.

There are two main errors in riding down steep hills; rider tension and postural faults. For the less experienced, a steep slope can be quite daunting, and tension can manifest itself to the horse via a stiff, tight seat, fiercely gripping legs and a heavy rein contact, all of which may disturb him both mentally and physically. Obviously, the more practise the rider has had on gentler slopes, the less likely is tension to manifest itself, but if it does, a conscious effort to keep calm and supple, and remembering to breathe, can all help. Also, talking soothingly to the horse may not only encourage him, but also have a reflected influence on the rider!

The main postural errors arise from a decision to lean either backwards or forwards taken in isolation from the demands of the actual circumstances.

Some riders adopt a 'defensive' posture, leaning back in the saddle, with legs thrust forward and a long, even loose, rein. Although it is possible to understand the self-preservation instinct behind this action, such a posture is hardly of assistance to the horse, since the rider becomes a mere passenger, and his weight distribution will be at best unhelpful, and, in more extreme cases, a real hindrance.

On the other hand, there are those who automatically lean forward with a vague intention of 'unburdening the hindquarters . While it is true that the horse will be making considerable use of his hocks and quarters, he can do so perfectly well with the rider sitting in a balanced position; an exaggerated shift of weight forward will merely serve to overburden the forehand instead. Indeed, the rider who forfeits the security of his position and gets in front of the horse's centre of gravity is not only putting himself in peril, but also hindering, rather than helping, his mount.

The cure for either 'leaning' fault is for the rider to concentrate on feeling that he is 'with' his horse, rather than slavishly following a preconception. To tackle a steep slope horse and rider must be in harmony, and this will not automatically result from the rider adhering to some magic formula regarding the angles of his body.

PREPARING TO WALK DOWN STEEP HILLS   Although it may seem a little back to front, I am dealing with the preparatory aspect *after* discussing the actual descent because I feel that, if the rider is unsure of what he is to do and expect when actually

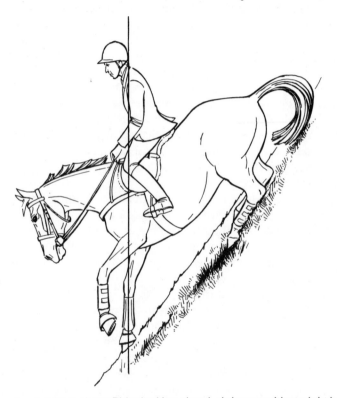

Riding down a steep slope. Rider looking ahead, sitting up with straight back. Elbow is 'soft', and there is a light contact with a good length of rein. Leg position is maintained. There is an impression of stillness and natural balance, with rider sitting deep in the saddle. Vertical line through rider's shoulder and knee, and horse's centre of gravity and foreleg, shows combined weight in optimum position. Horse's pricked ears indicate confidence. *Note:* in this illustration, horse is just about to move into canter to approach fence at foot of slope negotiating the hill, he will not be in the best frame of mind for preparing the horse.

The manner in which a horse makes such a descent is dictated by the quality of preparation as well as the ensuing riding down the hill itself. The key points are to establish a responsive walk with the horse between leg and hand, and to ride an approach in line with that of the intended descent, which should be straight down the hill.

Upon reaching the top of the hill, the horse may well pause momentarily, and this should not be discouraged, since it merely indicates that he is summing up the task before him. There should not, however, be a prolonged hesitation, and the horse should not be permitted to establish a halt; still less to step backwards. The rider should keep both legs on the horse with even, but not fierce, pressure, and politely insist that he moves forward down the hill. Any attempt on the horse's part to turn sideways must be firmly corrected, with the rider using his legs rather than hands. However, if the horse does succeed in turning significantly, he should be re-presented, with the rider using the knowledge of hindsight to avoid a repetition.

Horses do not, in fact, usually object unduly to tackling a hill, and severe nappiness is most likely in a young or untrained horse, or else one which is lame or has been badly ridden in the past. If substantial resistance *is* encountered, the rider should consider the likely cause, and whether the prevailing circumstances are such that compulsion is appropriate, or an easier route should be sought pending attention to the root of the problem. Offers of a 'lead' from another horse should be evaluated with care, in case the horse is tempted to hurry, and if the offer is accepted, the 'lead' should not be followed too closely.

TROTTING DOWNHILL Where the gradient is suitable, and there is a purpose to going faster than walk, trot is a useful gait to employ. The relatively short stride and diagonal nature of footfall assist the horse in keeping his balance; in fact horses who meet bad going or a downhill slope at canter will often change to trot of their own accord.

When trotting downhill, the basic principles of straightness, balance and contact apply as in walk. However, it is probably easier for the horse if the rider rises to the trot, as long as he remains in balance and does not bump down into the saddle. With practise, it is possible to achieve a 'rising' trot where the rider is poised above the saddle, and, in the 'sitting' phase, hardly brushes it with the seat of his breeches. The reader with experience of riding with pretty short leathers, either for jumping or galloping, will be aware of this sensation from moments of trotting with them so adjusted. The success of trotting in this fashion depends upon the rider's ability to rise from his thighs rather than the stirrups, and to retain his dynamic balance. Less experienced riders should, therefore, ensure that they can do so on the flat before attempting it downhill, in the interest of both themselves and their mount.

CANTER AND GALLOP DOWNHILL   It is quite possible, given good going and a moderate gradient, to ride downhill at these gaits. Indeed, anyone who has witnessed a field of young racehorses negotiating Tattenham Hill at Epsom will be amazed at just how possible it is. This does not, however, mean that it is easy; the jockeys at Epsom are professionals whose livelihood depends largely upon their ability to keep horses balanced when travelling flat out. The less experienced rider should, therefore, be prepared to work up to such feats in easy stages, and the essential preliminary requirements are the ability to descend hills in good style at the slower gaits, and to maintain control and balance at the faster gaits on level ground.

When the rider intends to canter down a hill, he should ensure that he has established the type of canter he wants before starting the descent, since it is very unlikely that he will be able to improve the gait, or his degree of control, once he meets the slope. The horse will naturally tend to quicken, and lengthen his stride downhill, but he will be less likely to do so, and to a lesser extent, if he is on a short, bouncy, and well-balanced stride to start with.

It should be borne in mind that the pace cannot be properly controlled by hanging on to the reins; this will only cause the horse go hollow and to 'lose' his back end and balance, so that he is virtually obliged to go faster still, creating an undesirable 'snowball' effect. The rider must, therefore, use his seat and legs to ensure that the horse remains in as rounded an outline as the

Galloping downhill

slope permits, and moves forward into the contact, which should be sensitive and 'alive' to any changes of outline and rein length which may result from variations in the gradient.

Galloping downhill is a different proposition, since the sequence of footfall (hind, hind, fore, fore) produces a very long stride, and, with the horse stretching his neck out to balance himself, he will be going in a very 'flat' outline. Clumsily ridden, or allowed to 'get away', his progress will become very precipitate, and he will reach the bottom of the slope flat out and completely out of contol. A horse may, then, break into gallop down a hill because he has not been ridden well enough in canter, or because the gradient is too steep for him to keep his balance, but these are problems best prevented by thoughtful and accurate riding, since they can hardly be solved once they have occurred. Galloping downhill by design may be appropriate at times; in the hunting field for instance, but in circumstances where there are jumps to be taken, or turns to negotiate, rather more measured progress is prudent.

37

If a rider decides to go down a (gentle) hill at gallop he should, in the interests of his own seat and balance, adopt an upper body posture rather more over the centre of motion (i.e. further back) than he would when galloping on the flat; and, while he should not ram his legs forward, it may be prudent to allow the lower leg to move a little in front of the girth. His position will be similar to the restraining posture, but the rein contact should be just sufficient to keep the horse on the bit, whilst enabling him to adopt his naturally preferred head carriage.

It should be borne in mind that horses galloping downhill go very fast, and a rider who panics in these circumstances and takes a stranglehold on the reins risks serious injury. The reader should, therefore, have reason to feel confident in his own ability and his surroundings before attempting this feat, especially if he is in company, when there is a risk of causing interference to other horses and riders.

RIDING ACROSS SLOPES   It is inevitable that there will be times when it is necessary to traverse the face of a slope. This is not very

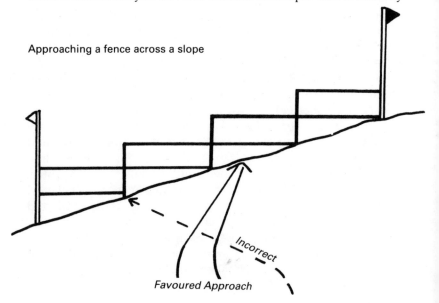

Approaching a fence across a slope

Incorrect

Favoured Approach

easy for the horse, who will have to adjust his movements in order to keep upright. These adjustments will invariably affect his gaits to some degree, and both horse and rider will need to check a natural tendency to drift down the hill.

The rider's best policy in these circumstances is to sit still and square in the saddle, interfering as little as possible, although it may be necessary for him to keep his 'downhill' leg rather more firmly on the girth. Changes of gait should be avoided as far as possible, and, where there is some choice of route, it makes sense to traverse the least steep part of the slope on the shortest possible line. Where a fence has to be jumped 'across' a slope, the rider should approach it as much 'uphill' as he can commensurate with meeting it at a reasonable angle, and should favour aiming for the 'uphill' side of the obstacle. This approach will be much easier for the horse than a 'downhill' one, and will lessen the temptation for him to run out down the hill.

3
Jumping

Mention of tackling fences across the face of slopes brings us to the topic of jumping which, for many people, is the epitome of riding cross-country. It is not, however, the be all and end all, and the reason for my devoting the first section of this book to the issues of control, and correct riding over undulating terrain is that, until the rider can perform efficiently in these areas, he is hardly being fair to himself or his horse if he attempts to tackle fences. This principle of getting it right on the 'flat' first applies to all types of jumping, but it is especially important across country where circumstances frequently dictate that obstacles be tackled at the faster gaits or on sloping ground.

Tackling Various Obstacles

Jumping cross-country is, in fact, very much about coping with practicalities, since all sorts of fences have to be negotiated in a wide variety of circumstances, many of which make the process far more awkward than will be experienced within the confines of the schooling arena. In any form of cross-country sport, the penalty for failure at a jump is likely to be severe. I am not talking here primarily of the risk of injury, but rather of the inherent nature of the game. In most types of cross-country competition the standard twenty penalties for a single refusal will be enough to keep a rider out of the placings, and a fall, incurring sixty penalties, will most definitely do so. In other areas, such as hunting, an untimely refusal may not only inconvenience the rider, but may also cause interference to others in the field. In any instance a horse running loose after a fall may take a good deal of retrieving, and, while free, is a potential hazard to other riders, spectators, crops, traffic and even himself.

Security and effectiveness are, therefore, prime considerations when jumping cross-country. The top three day event riders are not successful because of an ability to look photogenic when jumping large, but straightforward fences, but because they can stay in the saddle and get out of trouble in the most dire circumstances. To be secure and effective embraces various attributes: adaptability, determination, and the ability to communicate positively with the horse, and to retain his confidence. Purely on the physical side, requirements are a strong and adhesive seat, and the ability to readily adapt the posture to suit the demands of a particular obstacle. The basic techniques of jumping are examined in *Riding Over Jumps*, which makes the point that there is no one 'jumping position'. However, I feel it would be helpful to reiterate a little, and to look in more detail at the *types* of posture which the rider will need to adopt in order to cope safely and efficiently with various cross-country jumps.

NORMAL CIRCUMSTANCES By 'normal', I am referring to any situation where the rider is tackling a fairly straightforward fence on more or less level ground. However, this description still embraces a number of variable conditions. These are, chiefly:

1) The actual approach to the fence may be tricky, e.g. limited in distance, or down a winding path.
2) The gait and speed of approach can vary from steady trot to strong gallop.
3) Ground conditions may be less than ideal.
4) The horse may be tired.
5) The rider may be tired.
6) The fence may be taken in company, increasing emphasis on control.

These conditions are by no means mutually exclusive; they can, in fact, be pretty comprehensively permutated. The type of posture required for jumping 'normal' cross-country fences has, then, to be such that the rider is ready and able to cope with all contingencies. He must ride a strong enough approach to prevent refusals, be secure enough not to fall off if the horse hits the fence or stumbles, and be in good enough balance with the horse to assist/allow him to recover in such circumstances. Furthermore, he must be able to make each jump as easy and comfortable for the horse as possible, bearing in mind that every fence taken well is a mutual confidence builder, enhancing the degree of rapport upon which it may be necessary to draw heavily on other occasions. Faults to avoid are drawing the lower leg back behind the girth, raising the seat high out of the saddle and folding further forward than is required to stay in harmony with the horse's movement. These errors tend to be related to the serious error of anticipating the jump, mentioned earlier. It is also important that the hands are not tucked into the horse's neck or wither, since hands and arms must remain free to do their share of 'allowing', and the rider must always be in a position where he is able to slip the reins instantly in the event of difficulties.

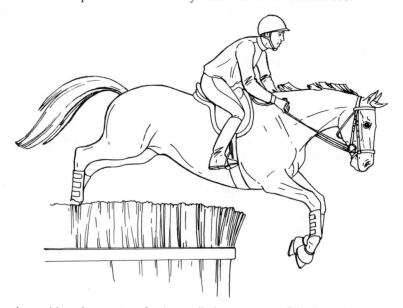

A good jumping posture for 'normal' circumstances. Rider's position very secure, sitting closely 'into' horse, whilst folding forward sufficiently to go 'with' his effort; hands and arms follow movement of horse's head and neck. The impression is that, if the horse put in a sudden stop, hit the fence or stumbled on landing, the rider's position would remain much the same

'DROPS' A 'drop' is an obstacle where the landing side is lower than the take-off side. Examples include fences dividing fields of different levels, jumps into sunken lanes or water, fences taken downhill and 'steps' (jumps which consist of going from a higher to a lower level with no actual fence involved).

When a horse takes a drop fence, he will land at a steeper angle than if he jumped a similar fence on level ground. This is because his jump will follow an arc, established on the take-off side, with the line of his body describing, broadly speaking, a series of tangents to that arc. If the arc is extended below the 'normal' landing point, the angle between his body and the ground will increase. The steeper landing will cause a greater degree of deceleration than usual, both because of the increased effects of gravity, and because the angle of landing will affect the speed and facility with which the horse can initially use his legs to regain his forward momentum. Obviously, the bigger the fence and the greater the drop, the more these factors will come into play.

The rider's problem is how to cope with the influences of steep landing and deceleration upon his own security, while still making the jump as easy as possible for the horse; if he adopts and retains a posture suitable for taking a similar fence on level ground, the steeper landing will result in his upper body being at too acute an angle to the ground, and the impact of landing will pitch him still further forward. It is for this reason that riders who have been taught that there is one correct 'jumping position' approach drops with trepidation.

The solution to the problem lies in the principle of not allowing oneself to get in front of the centre of gravity, especially at the moment of landing. In fact, because of the effects of deceleration, which cannot be precisely prejudged, and the self preservation factor, which should include some contingency for if the horse stumbles, it is prudent to think in terms of being slightly behind the centre of gravity on landing. Although the actual circumstances of each jump will vary somewhat, a basic 'rule of thumb' for converting this theory into practice is to ensure that the upper body is pretty much vertical to *the ground* by the moment of landing. The practical way to do this is to assume such a vertical posture once the horse has reached the highest point of his jumping arc (with a step down, this will be the moment after take-

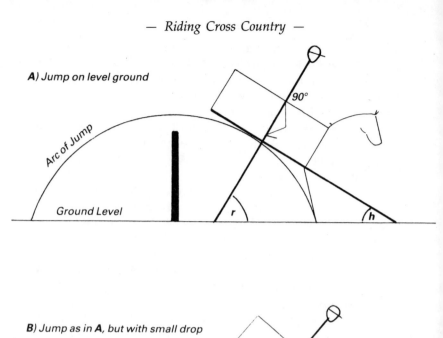

A) *Jump on level ground*

Arc of Jump

Ground Level

90°

r

h

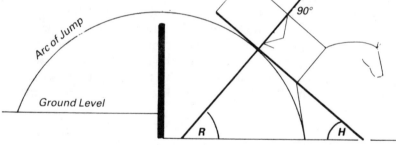

B) *Jump as in **A**, but with small drop*

Arc of Jump

Ground Level

90°

R

H

The geometry of 'drop' jumps. (Rider's postures illustrated are intended as comparative examples only.) Even where only a small drop is involved (example shown is 25 per cent of height of fence), there is a significant impact on the key angles of descent. In diagram B, the angle between horse's body and the ground (H) is considerably steeper than corresponding angle (h) in diagram A. In both diagrams, rider's upper body is shown at 90° to horse, but the angle between rider's upper body and ground (R and r) is more acute over the drop.

off). This procedure will be made easier and smoother if the rider avoids asking his horse to 'stand off' and make an extravagant leap (which will not, in any case, help the horse's cause over a drop), and if he himself avoids any extravagance of posture during the first phase of the jump.

As the rider assumes his vertical posture, his hands will automatically move back further from the horse's mouth. Any attempt to avoid this by sticking the arms out like ramrods is undesirable, both because it will introduce stiffness, and because the extra rein provided will be offered jerkily, and may not, in any case, be of sufficient length. The correct, and essential procedure is then, that the reins are slipped quickly and smoothly, allowing the horse to take as much rein as he requires. If the reins are not slipped correctly, the horse will be jabbed in the mouth and seriously unbalanced on landing, and the rider may well be pulled over his head, especially over a large drop or when jumping into water. The technique of slipping the reins is described in detail in *Riding Over Jumps*, and it is most important to be able to do so proficiently before attempting drop fences.

The final postural alteration over drops concerns the leg position. Any tendency for the lower leg to move backwards spells disaster at drop fences, but it may be appropriate for the leg to come forward during the descent phase. With the upper body upright, and the descent steep, it becomes rather unnatural to keep the leg on the girth. Also, such a position will do little to absorb the shock of landing. The rider should not automatically ram his legs forward, which will merely lock the knee and ankle joints and tend to push him up out of the saddle, but neither should he fight any natural tendency for the legs to swing forward so that the ankle joint is vertically beneath his hips and shoulders, with knee and ankle remaining flexed. It will be noted that such a posture actually corresponds closely to a 'normal' riding position on the flat; the rider is not really leaning back, but the circumstances of the jump are 'tilting' the horse forward.

REVERSE DROPS/STEPS UP Many obstacles which are encountered as drops or steps down can also be taken from the opposite direction, turning them into reverse drops or steps up. It is probably true to say that most such obstacles are easier to negotiate 'going up' but, despite being the exact opposite of drops, they have one thing in common with them, which is that the landing point is in a different position to that in a jump on level ground; in this case, abnormally early in the jumping arc.

The nature of such obstacles is such that the horse will usually be able to see the landing point in advance, and will tend to allow for this on the approach, seeking to arrive at the take-off point on a fairly short stride with his hocks beneath him. This is something that the rider should actively encourage (up a manufactured flight of steps, he may get some help from the course builder), ensuring that the stride remains short and active, and that the horse does not just slow down.

Taking a drop jump. Rider in vertical posture. Elbows flexed – hands starting to 'slip' reins. Lower leg vertically beneath upper body, retaining some flexion in knee and ankle. Posture looks very secure, but does not give any impression of being forced or 'defensive'

In the early stages of such a jump the horse will, if he is jumping off a good stride, elevate quite steeply, requiring that the rider folds forward considerably in order to go 'with' him, rather as when going up a steep hill. It is important that the rider does not get behind the centre of gravity at this stage, since, if the jump is a 'step' and the horse lands a little short, he may initially have to rely on his forehand to pull himself forward, and this will be made considerably more difficult if the rider is sitting unduly far back. On the other hand, it is important that the rider does not get in front of the centre of gravity, or he will be caught out by the 'early' finish to the jump, like a car passenger being plunged forward by sudden and unexpected braking. This problem may be compounded if the horse jumps boldly and lands well, since the angle of the jump will cause his quarters to engage earlier than usual, and the thrust of the initial 'move away' stride may cause the saddle to give the unbalanced rider a whack in the backside, which will not help matters.

The issue of rein contact is, once again, very important. The combination of steep take-off and the rider's folding will tend to shorten the distance between hand and bit, but this will be followed by a need to lengthen the rein as the horse stretches his neck on landing. Obviously, there is no time to physically shorten and lengthen the reins so, in order to maintain a contact, the rider may find that he flexes the elbows outwards as a means of 'absorbing' the initial 'shortening', before allowing his hands and forearms to move forward in response to the horse's change of outline on landing. 'Sticking the elbows out' is sometimes cited as a fault in jumping and, where it is perceived as a habit in the school arena, this may well be the case. In the circumstances under discussion, however, it is a practical means of retaining the contact, and is frequently practised under competition conditions by top event riders. As with all jumping, then, harmony is of the essence over reverse drops, but the nature of such obstacles highlights the presence, or lack, of this quality. Taken well, such jumps are generally straightforward, but, taken badly, they can result in an undignified scramble.

BANKS   These are usually natural obstacles, and appear in great profusion in certain areas, especially in Ireland. They are roughly

(This page and opposite.)

Take-off and landing at a step up

dome-shaped in cross-section, sometimes faced with stone, often covered in scrub, and frequently have ditches on one or both sides. They are best tackled by combining the principles of taking reverse drops and riding uphill while 'going up', and of riding downhill and taking drops when 'going down'. These processes have to be followed in rapid succession and, indeed, the horse taking a small bank may merely jump onto the top, sort his legs out, and jump off the other side. Banks are, therefore, excellent 'practise' obstacles for both rider and horse, but the more formidable are best tackled after gaining initial experience of the underlying principles involved.

NATURAL DITCHES AND STREAMS   Ditches are always to be treated with considerable respect. Where artificial or 'tidied-up' versions, with secure take-off and landing, are met in the course of competitive events, they are usually best ridden as though

they were formidable fences of 'normal' construction. However, when natural ditches and streams are encountered, a different approach may be called for, since the banks may be ill-defined, muddy, unlevel, or even inclined to crumble under the weight of horse and rider.

Galloping at such features is a sure formula for getting wet and muddy, and also increases the risk of tendon injuries, etc., to the horse. They must be treated as obstacles to negotiate, rather than 'jumps', and the prudent rider will trot, or even walk, towards them, using his legs firmly to retain the impulsion and convey his intentions to the horse.

This is one instance where it can be appropriate for the rider to fold forward in advance of take-off, the reasons being:
1) The horse will be moving quite slowly, and, if he does stop, the effect on a rider who has folded forward correctly should be minimal. Since such obstacles are not normally met in

competition, the problem of penalties does not arise, and neither should that of hampering other riders, since it is foolish to get too close in such circumstances.

2) With such obstacles, the take-off point and moment have to be assessed by the horse rather than the rider, so the chances of moving completely in harmony during the jump are somewhat curtailed.

3) Notwithstanding this, it is important that the rider does not get 'left behind', the reasons being similar to those mentioned in connection with steps up, though perhaps more complex. Apart from uncertainties about the ground in the take-off area, and the effectiveness of the thrust which the horse can generate from a poor footing, there are also potential landing problems. The horse may, perforce, land on the upslope of the far bank, perhaps in slippery mud, or even on ground which gives way. In such an event, he will need to make maximum use of his forehand to pull himself into a position from which he can obtain purchase with his hind limbs, and he will be greatly assisted if the rider's weight is well forward over the centre of gravity. The rider who is comprehensively 'left behind' at a moment like this may hamper his horse to the extent that he is unable to negotiate the ditch successfully, and slips backwards into the bottom.

When taking such jumps, the horse tends to accelerate suddenly from a virtual standstill into a flat trajectory, with a considerable lengthening of his neck. On landing, he may keep his neck in a long outline whilst seeking to establish his balance. It is therefore most important that the rider's hands are kept free to follow the movement and/or slip the reins, and this is an instance where there is no real harm in surrendering the contact for a moment.

Jumping Into and Out of Water

Basically, this involves the techniques of jumping drops and reverse drops, but the additional factor is the water itself, which exerts a considerable braking effect, both on landing, and when travelling through it.

If an obstacle in competition involves going into water, the state of the stream or lake bed, and the depth along and around the proposed route, should be checked when walking the course, so remember to do your course-walking in waterproof boots! In non-competitive circumstances, it is best to follow someone familiar with the country, or at least someone who hasn't sunk without trace, but it is important not to get too close behind them.

It is generally maintained that the best way to jump into water is from the slowest possible approach, so that the effects of deceleration are minimised. Unfortunately, riders who stick slavishly to the letter of this principle can get into trouble because they go too slowly and with no impulsion; this happens especially on occasions where there is a fence to be jumped on the way in. It must be remembered that to jump even a small fence requires a reasonable degree of impulsion, and, if the horse takes a dislike to the water and starts to 'back off' during the approach, then the initial amount of impulsion has to be quite high in order for there to be anything left for take-off. The horse who comes to a virtual standstill before responding reluctantly to the urgings of his rider often lands in a heap in the water or, worse still, 'leaves a leg' on the jump in, and tips up on landing.

One year I spent a long time at the Burghley Horse Trials watching competitors at the 'Trout Hatchery', one of the most famous water obstacles in the eventing world. A point which became apparent was that the majority of riders who approached very slowly and with no discernible impulsion experienced refusals or falls, whereas the majority of riders who apparently approached a little too fast, but with some degree of 'bounce' got away with it, even if not in classical style. I should qualify this observation by reporting that the best results came from those who approached steadily, but with great energy (i.e. with collection), while those who came in fast and flat were tipped up by the braking effect of the water. However, it does seem that if the criteria of retaining impulsion and going slowly are assessed in isolation, then retaining impulsion appears to be the more important and effective measure. Furthermore, as with all difficult and uninviting jumps, it must be remembered that a refusal still leaves you on the wrong side of the fence, with twenty penalties, a negative horse, and no guarantee of success on the next attempt.

While it is impossible to generalise on the best gait for

approaching jumps into water, a properly collected canter or an active trot will cover most circumstances, and the active trot is frequently easier to establish.

Once safely in the water, the rider may have to jump either another obstacle in it, or one on the way out. Although some horses will try and rush through shallow water, it should be remembered that it is much harder for the horse to go forward in these conditions than on dry land, and the stride will be shorter than usual (try running through the shallow end of your local swimming baths). Since it is not possible to foresee precisely what effect the water will have on the length of stride, it is inadvisable to try and 'ride strides' as if going through a combination on dry land. The sensible procedure is to pick a route which will give the horse some room to recover if he lands in a heap on entry, and, once in, to ride him firmly but not frantically forward on as straight an approach as possible, waiting for the jump 'to come to you'. Horses rarely 'stand off' when jumping from water, but they seldom refuse to jump out of it onto dry land, unless their task is made virtually impossible.

First Cross-Country Jumps

For the less experienced rider, this talk of drops, ditches and water jumps may seem somewhat high-flown. However, the reason for examining the varied possibilities of jumping cross-country before reverting to basics is to give the reader an idea of what he should be aiming towards, so that he is not progressing in the dark. Initial attempts at cross-country style fences should be made under instruction, on a steady, honest horse, and the first step is to get used to the idea of solid jumps. For some people, this represents no problem at all, but for others, the transition from knock-down poles to creosoted sleepers and the like can be somewhat daunting. Since such jumps are an integral part of most cross-country courses, however, the transition should be made as promptly and comprehensively as possible.

Introductory fences should be sited on level ground and good going, should present as wide a face as possible, and be tackled free of secondary problems such as riding away from the direction of home or other horses. They should be small, about

0·6m (2ft) high, but of solid construction and imposing appearance. Such fences are, in fact, about the easiest a horse can ever be asked to jump, since they are easy to see and weigh up, and encourage a bold, clean leap. The novice rider will, however, be much more convinced of this after having taken a number without fuss.

Once familiar with, and confident over, such obstacles, the rider should be introduced to the practical importance of retaining control and impulsion and 'making room' when tackling awkwardly sited jumps. Since the emphasis here is on approach and landing, and the rider may well make initial errors, the jumps themselves, while still needing to be recognisable as such, should be rather more forgiving; piles of brushwood and small fallen trees fitting the bill.

Jumps sited just before or after turns in woodland paths will encourage thoughtful, accurate riding, and an ensuing exercise is for the rider to take a jump built on a well-defined track, and then promptly turn off onto a more minor path. In order to control the horse's natural desire to quicken down the obvious route on landing, the rider must be well in command on the approach, and make good, clear application of leg and direct rein aids immediately after the jump, still thinking of riding forwards.

I recall being taken on 'instructional hacks', and being sent ducking under branches and weaving through the undergrowth in order to jump naturally occurring obstacles from perhaps two or three strides of trot. This is very good practise for the cross-country rider, and helps explode the myth, common amongst novice riders, that fences need to be approached fast and from long range.

When confidence and control have been consolidated, the rider is ready for his experience to be steadily widened to include jumping up and down hill, taking small drops, and progressing to larger and more difficult jumps on level ground. After this, it is largely a question of gaining knowledge and effectiveness through practise, since the basics remain much the same from novice level to the highest grade. Participating in local and club level competitions can be very helpful at this stage, since the rider has to make use of his own abilities without guidance from an instructor (although access to a knowledgeable friend before and after competing is most useful). Good performances in these circumstances act as a considerable morale booster, while the wise rider will also appreciate the value of analysing, and learning from, mistakes. There is, however, one further technical issue which should be given consideration, and that is the ability to appreciate, and influence, the stride upon which the horse meets his fences.

Seeing a Stride

Being able to 'see a stride' is often considered primarily as a virtue of the show-jumper. Whilst it is undoubtedly essential for anyone wishing to proceed beyond novice level in that discipline, it is also very important across country, notwithstanding the exceptional circumstances mentioned in jumping from water. The emphasis differs somewhat between show-jumping and cross-country. In the former, horse and rider are performing on level ground, jumping relatively large, knock-down fences with related distances between them, and the principle is to establish an even, rounded stride, and to lengthen or shorten according to the perceived demands of the course builder. As we have seen with cross country, the terrain may be anything but level, gait, speed and stride length are subject to change, and obstacles often occur where nature, or deceased farmers, happened to place them. Indeed, in some situations, a 'good' stride will not exist, and the earlier this is recognised the more chance there is to alter the approach, or, more probably, make the best of the route which has been chosen (or thrust upon one).

The ability to foresee where and when the horse is likely to take-off is, then, a valuable asset, both from the point of view of efficiency and safety. Unfortunately, this is an area where many novice riders are weak; there is a general assumption that knowledge of striding is a mystery revealed only to international show-jumpers and instructors, and few novice riders will bother to pace out (or even look at) the distance through a combination when walking a course. Furthermore, despite the common teaching exercise of counting the last three strides into a fence (which most riders will experience under instruction), many appear not to put the experience into practice to any degree when performing alone, and frequently get comprehensively caught out if the horse 'stands off' or 'fiddles' a jump.

It may, therefore, be useful to look in some detail at the various ways in which a horse can approach and meet a fence, to assist the reader in understanding the principles behind good and bad strides, and thus recognising them when they occur. There are two basic factors which influence how a horse meets a jump: the take-off zone and the horse's own stride.

TAKE-OFF ZONE Although terrain and going have some influence upon the take-off zone, it is chiefly determined by the construction of the fence itself, especially its vertical height. Assuming a fairly level approach and landing, reasonable ground, and a jump which is not of extraordinary height or spread, the take-off zone is classically reckoned to be between 1 and 1½ times the maximum height of the fence from a spot vertically beneath its highest point. For example, the take-off zone for an upright fence 0·9m (3ft) high would be between 0.9 and 1·35m (3ft and 4½ft) from its base. In practical terms, however, providing the horse is operating well within the limit of his capabilities, this zone can be extended to about twice the maximum height of the fence from beneath its highest point.

As a general rule, when jumping drops, sloping spreads (e.g. triple bar type jumps), steps, larger uprights, and most fences considered awkward by the rider, it is preferable to take-off from the part of the zone nearer to the fence. This also applies when jumping out of heavy going, which requires extra effort on the horse's part, and on hard ground, where a less extravagant leap may save the horse from undue jarring.

Where relatively easy fences (most hedges and brush jumps, and small, straightforward obstacles) are met on a long stride, taking off from the 'far' part of the zone may produce a more fluent leap. Should a fence have a ditch on the take-off side, the option may be limited to that portion of the zone which is above ground! Also, when approaching fences downhill, it is preferable not to get too close to the base of the fence, since this will effectively increase its height, and require extra effort from the horse to elevate his forehand.

These variations are, however, ideas more applicable to the

fairly experienced rider tackling bigger courses, and the aim is, initially, to place the horse somewhere within the take-off zone. Failure to do so does not *necessarily* mean that the fence cannot be jumped; it is a question of degree and circumstance, as we shall see shortly.

STRIDE Within each gait, the horse will have an optimum stride length, which he will adopt when travelling at his 'cruising speed', and a practical maximum and minimum stride length. These will all be influenced by conditions, and will vary from horse to horse. The optimum stride will be, broadly speaking, an average length, from which the horse will be able to either lengthen or shorten. It follows, however, that he can only adjust his stride from its maximum by shortening, and from its minimum by lengthening. There is, then, more potential for adjustment if the horse approaches a fence on his optimum stride, but this will not always be practical or desirable. For instance, shorter strides will be favoured if the fence is awkwardly sited, or if the construction of the obstacle requires them (e.g. series of steps, or 'bounce' fence with a tight distance). Longer strides will be appropriate when tackling straightforward fences when there is an accent on speed, and will also be, to some extent, a product of downhill approaches.

However, the principle of being able to adjust the stride 'both ways' should be borne in mind, and approaching jumps at completely full stretch, or with maximum collection, should be avoided wherever possible. Although, as we shall see, adjusting the stride length is closely linked with 'seeing a stride', attempting drastic adjustments when close to a fence should be avoided, as should habitual fiddling around 'looking for a stride'. The reasons for this are:

1) It may merely confuse the horse, especially if he has 'summed up' the fence himself, in a different fashion from the rider.
2) It is time-consuming; a drawback in many forms of cross-country riding.
3) In company, it may cause interference to others, or allow/ provoke them into passing, and unsighting, you.

This is not to say that some obstacles do not require careful setting up and "show-jumping", but these are relatively scarce, and the horse is more likely to respond obediently to the rider on such occasions if he is not habitually pulled around at every jump.

Putting the factors of take-off zone and stride together, we can come to a definition of a good stride being one where the horse, approaching with as smooth a rhythm as possible, arrives within the take-off zone. (At a more advanced stage, the favoured part of the take-off zone.) An indifferent stride is one which places the horse just beyond the fringes of the take-off zone, and/or involves some stride adjustment at a late stage. A bad stride is one which causes the horse to miss the take-off zone altogether, or calls for drastic last moment adjustments to get within its fringes. If a horse meets a jump on a bad stride, he has the following options: if he is too close to the fence, and it is small, he may be able to scramble over it; if he senses he is going to meet a fence wrong, an experienced and resourceful horse may either break his rhythm and gait in the final yards of approach and 'fiddle' his way over or 'stand off', i.e. take-off abnormally far from the fence.

Should he be unable or unwilling to pursue any of these options, he will either refuse or run-out. Many refusals and run-outs are, in fact, caused either by the rider driving his horse (or letting him run) at a fence flat out, or else overchecking and losing impulsion, so that the horse reaches the fence on an impossible stride.

The first stage of actually seeing a stride is being able to recognise, on the last stride before take-off, whether it is good, indifferent or bad, and, if bad, whether the horse is going to be too close or too far from the fence. This ability at least gives the rider a moment to react, and may make the difference between getting safely over the jump and having a fall. It can be learnt by practice and experience, both in and out of the school, and it is a good idea to make a point, whenever jumping, or trying to assess how the fence will be met, and asking oneself afterwards whether the assessment was right or wrong, and why.

However, once this initial ability is established, the rider will find, with continuing experience, that he can see the stride a little further away. This is a real bonus because he need no longer merely react at the last moment; he will be in a position to actually influence the approach for the better, and turn a potentially bad stride into a perfectly satisfactory one, without resorting to

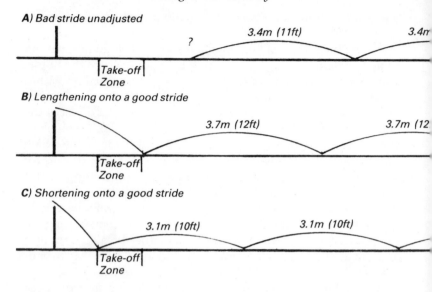

A) *Bad stride unadjusted*

?   3.4m (11ft)   3.4m

Take-off Zone

B) *Lengthening onto a good stride*

3.7m (12ft)   3.7m (12

Take-off Zone

C) *Shortening onto a good stride*

3.1m (10ft)   3.1m (10ft)

Take-off Zone

Seeing and riding onto a stride

drastic measures. To establish the truth of this, and highlight the usefulness of seeing a stride, let us look at an example:

Let us take the 0·9m (3ft) high upright, and remember that its take-off zone is between 0·9 and 1·8m (3 and 6ft) from its base. Suppose a horse approaching this fence has a practical maximum stride length of 3·9m (13ft), and a practical minimum stride length of 2·8m (9ft) (these figures are not intended to be definitive), and is approaching on a 3·4m (11ft) stride, which would be somewhere around his optimum. If the horse arrived at a point 2·8m (9ft) from the base of the fence, he would be on a thoroughly bad stride; a long way away to 'stand off', and too close to do anything but put in an extremely short shuffle.

If we move the horse back one stride, he will be 6·1m (20ft) from the fence, which is a little more promising. If horse and rider realise the problem at this juncture, there is the option of putting in one maximum stride, which will leave them 2·1m (7ft) from the fence, or two minimum strides, which will leave them 0·6m (2ft) from it. Either choice *might* enable them to negotiate the jump successfully, although both require fairly drastic action. This 'first

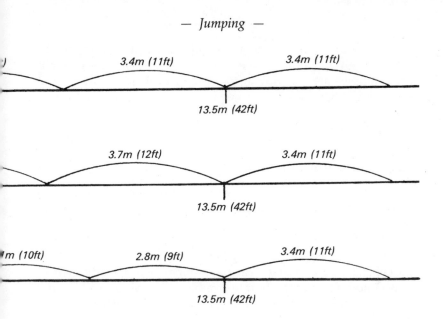

stage' in seeing a stride is, however, demonstrably better than not seeing one at all.

Suppose, though, we move the horse back another two strides, so that he is a total of 12·9m (42ft) from the fence. If the rider realises at this juncture that the approach is potentially wrong, he has both room to adjust it and options as to how he does so. Should the fence be one which can happily be met on a longish stride, he can lengthen into it, for instance taking three 3·7m (12ft) strides, which would bring the horse 1·8m (6ft) from the fence, on the edge of the take off zone. Slightly longer strides would, of course, take him further into the heart of the zone.

If it is more appropriate to meet the fence on a short stride, the rider can, at this juncture, check/collect the horse, so that he takes one minimum 2·8m (9ft) stride, and then ask him to go on a little more, perhaps taking three 3·1m (10ft) strides, bringing him to a point 0·9m (3ft) from the fence, an appropriate take-off point for a jump requiring to be met rather 'short'.

In both examples, alterations in stride length are quite slight, and the one more pronounced alteration – the checking stride in the second example – is carried out at the start of the approach, and not right in front of the fence. (The exact distances given in the examples are, of course, for ease of explanation.) I am not suggesting that the reader need turn himself into a human theodolite, but I am suggesting that he can cultivate something of an eye and 'feel' for distance, and will benefit by so doing.

Reconnaissance of Striding

The obstacles mentioned earlier that require special attention to striding are usually combinations of some sort, met during competition, having been designed by the course-builder to test the riders judgement and accuracy of presentation. Since course-builders, even at local level, are being increasingly influenced by the construction of obstacles at major horse trials, it is advisable to pay a good deal of attention to combinations when walking the course, especially those offering alternative routes. Such obstacles can only be ridden as well as they have been assessed, and assessment will include asking and answering the following questions:

HOW MANY ELEMENTS ARE THERE? A very basic question, but it should be remembered that the more elements there are, the more mental and physical effort required, and the greater the importance of initial impulsion and adherence to the chosen line.

BETWEEN ELEMENTS We need here to ask the question: What is the striding like between elements, bearing in mind my horse's likely stride length in the prevailing conditions? There are two points to consider:
1) Do not allow yourself to become hidebound by theoretical 'correct' distances. These are usually based on the assumption of onward-bound horses jumping biggish fences on good, level going. If you are riding a stuffy little cob round a 0·8m (2½ft) course in the mud, they will be nothing but misleading. Obviously, if you are riding an animal with whom your acquaintance is limited, you will be at some disadvantage here, but, providing you have at least seen and sat on him, you should be able to make a reasonable estimate of his likely length of stride.

2) Never assume that distances between different elements are equal: pace them out. Also, do not be tempted to adjust your paces to accommodate wishful thinking.

With bounce fences there is, of course, no stride between elements, but the distance is still very important. Where there is a choice of distances (i.e. the elements are not parallel) accurate assessment and riding are especially important. If undecided as to the best line, it is probably wise to opt for a slightly longer, rather than shorter distance, since the horse may find it easier to reach a little for the second element rather than overshorten. My own experience is that longer striding horses who tend to 'make ground' through combinations need rather more room in a bounce than one might think, even when presented on a good 'rounded' stride. This is probably because the nature of bounce fences makes it pretty well essential to ride them quite strongly, and such horses tend to respond by making extra effort.

Small bounce fences with short distances are potentially more dangerous than bigger, longer ones, if an on-going horse is allowed to run at them. If he jumps in too far, he will get too close to the second element to jump out, and will either stop very suddenly, or hit the second element hard with his forelegs and risk a very nasty fall. Since both options are highly undesirable, it is essential not to allow yourself to get 'carted' into such a fence, and if there appears to be a risk of this happening, it is much safer to approach from trot, once this gait has been firmly established. Bounces and other combinations should, however, always be tackled with plenty of *impulsion*, both because of the athleticism they demand from the horse, and because, depending upon their actual construction, they may be quite difficult to escape from once you get marooned in the middle!

ARE THE ELEMENTS IN A STRAIGHT LINE? They may well not be; 'staggered' combinations, sited, as it were, on a bend in the course are quite commonplace, with the individual elements being angled somewhat like wheel spokes. With such an obstacle, it is necessary to look for a straight line through since, with perhaps four jumps to be taken in very quick succession, neither horse nor rider will be able to concentrate upon maintaining a bend. It is, of course, most important to ensure that

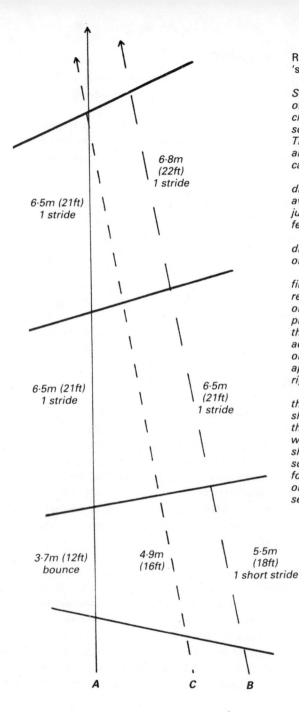

6·8m
(22ft)
1 stride

6·5m (21ft)
1 stride

6·5m (21ft)
1 stride

6·5m
(21ft)
1 stride

3·7m (12ft)
bounce

4·9m
(16ft)

5·5m
(18ft)
1 short stride

A   C   B

Routes through a 'staggered' combination.

Such obstacles usually offer some legitimate choice of route, and some 'no-go' routes. Thoughtful assessment and accurate riding are called for.

The distances in the diagram are based on an average 'school' horse jumping fairly small fences.

Route A provides good distances for bounce, one stride, one stride.

Route B offers a short first stride, with a requirement to lengthen on through, but could prove satisfactory if there were a significant advantage in time-saving or ground conditions in approaching from the right.

Route C — straight through the middle — should be avoided, as the first interval is wrong: even if a very short stride could be squeezed in, impulsion for the remainder of the obstacle would be severely impaired the chosen route offers a reasonable stride to each element, and it is preferable if the route does not start or finish too close to the end of a jump, so that the possibility of a run-out is avoided.

IS THERE AN OPTIONAL ELEMENT? Sometimes unflagged elements appear in combinations. These can either be jumped or missed out, according to the rider's wishes, and a fall or refusal at such a jump is penalised only in respect of the time it adds to the round. Depending upon the construction and layout of the combination, and its relationship to the general line of the course, jumping an unflagged section may improve the line through, or speed it up. However, it is not unknown for course-builders to introduce an unflagged jump which looks, superficially, tempting, but is actually a trap for the unwary, since it gives a bad stride to the next part of the obstacle proper. If, then, the rider feels that there is an advantage to be gained by jumping an optional element he should, for the purposes of course-walking, treat it as an integral part of the obstacle.

HOW ARE THE ELEMENTS NUMBERED? That is, is it really a combination (12A, B, C, etc.), or a series of separate fences close together (12, 13, 14)? This question does not directly affect the striding, but it does affect the allocation of penalties and may, therefore, have a bearing on how the obstacle must be retaken after a refusal. This is something which even the most positive rider should be aware of when course-walking, so that contingency plans can be formulated in order to keep any disasters as minimal as possible.

It is, of course, possible to meet combination fences in the course of non-competitive sport; for example, an 'in-and-out' through a lane. Since such obstacles were originally designed to allow the passage of carts rather than to provide a good stride, the distances may well be 'odd', and can catch out the rider who has not had the benefit of foresight. However, there is usually some alternative route, and a 'stop' in such circumstances will not have the impact upon the day's sport that it would in a competition. Nonetheless, the more experience the rider has of assessing and riding tricky combinations in competition, the more likely he is to either foresee the difficulty and somehow avoid it, or else to engineer a route through by controlled riding.

When it all Goes Wrong

However much one reads about seeing strides, and spends time studying general technique, there are those occasions in cross-country when everything goes wrong, and you meet a jump not only on a terrible stride, but with no contact, one stirrup and your backside on the cantle of the saddle. The reasons for this may be many and various; the most common is rider error in some form, but there are times when both he and the horse will be blameless. Whatever the cause, this is the moment when, as Col Frank Weldon says: 'The good cross-country horse will jump in spite of the rider.'

There are two main factors which will influence the horse in these circumstances; how he is usually ridden (which will have a major bearing on whether he is a good cross-country horse), and whether it is physically possible for him to attempt the jump. The bold, honest horse who is usually well-ridden and has confidence in his rider and himself will generally 'have a go' within the bounds of possibility, but the horse who is used to being 'let down' or interfered with in normal circumstances is going to say 'no thank you'.

The second factor, physical possibility, depends partly upon circumstances, and partly upon the rider. Since horses cannot levitate, there will be times when they just cannot jump a fence, but there will be other distinctly unpromising occasions when they can work wonders if encouraged and allowed to do so. There are three main points for the rider to bear in mind when in trouble:

1) Try to sit still. Even if you are in a distinctly unclassical and unhelpful position, it will be easier for the horse if your weight remains relatively stable than if you are flapping about like a stranded fish.

2) Give the horse enough rein. He will have enough on his plate without the added burden of being pulled in the mouth by an unbalanced rider, and this may be the critical factor governing whether or not he makes a successful jump. Although automatically 'throwing the reins at the horse' may not be necessary, this is one circumstance where retaining the contact should not be a prime consideration.

3) Give the horse as much encouragement as possible. Even if your legs are not in the prescribed position, put them on whatever part of the horse they will reach. It may also be surprisingly helpful to use the voice, although this should be done in encouraging, confident tones, and not take the form of a panic-stricken shriek!

The final point to remember, assuming that the horse gets you both out of difficulty, is to show your appreciation as soon as possible with a pat and a kind word. It should be borne in mind that, although horses are not over-endowed with emotions or intellectual powers, they do respond positively to encouragement and reward and, in any case, if your mount has just gone to extraordinary lengths to avoid sitting on you in a ditch, he deserves some sort of thanks.

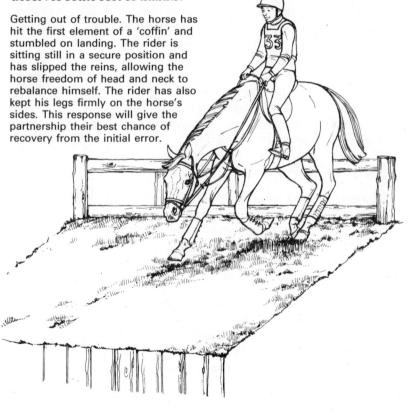

Getting out of trouble. The horse has hit the first element of a 'coffin' and stumbled on landing. The rider is sitting still in a secure position and has slipped the reins, allowing the horse freedom of head and neck to rebalance himself. The rider has also kept his legs firmly on the horse's sides. This response will give the partnership their best chance of recovery from the initial error.

4

Dealing With Natural Features and Conditions

If one is to ride across country, one must be able to deal not only with natural jumps, but also with other natural features and hazards as they occur. These are often more of a problem in non-competitive riding, since the rider may come upon them quite unexpectedly whereas, in competitive circumstances, there is the opportunity for course-walking. Also, of course, conscientious competition organisers will take pains to avoid including truly dangerous or unfair features in their course. However, in all cross-country riding, it is important to look ahead with a view to avoiding troublesome hazards, and also to know best to deal with those which cannot be avoided.

Fording Rivers and Streams

This is a common requirement of cross-country riding. Generally speaking, trained horses will go through water with little or no fuss, and some seem to actually enjoy doing so.

There are, however, some points the reader should be wary of, especially in unfamiliar country and we look at some of these below:

ARTIFICIAL IMPEDIMENTS   It is not unusual in these enlightened times for waterways to be treated as rubbish tips, and it is, therefore, unwise to charge headlong into water (especially if it is not clear) without looking to ensure that your horse is not about to entangle his legs in a discarded pram chassis.

BANKS   Some banks can be very treacherous – either slippery or crumbling – and, where possible, it pays to look for the most solid entry and exit points available.

LOOSE BOULDERS Particularly in upland areas, river beds are often strewn with loose, weed encrusted, boulders. These do not only give a very insecure footing in themselves, they may be perched on smaller stones, and rock alarmingly when stepped on. A horse, especially if young or unused to the area, may become seriously alarmed if marooned on such a boulder, and will normally 'freeze' and tremble. In such circumstances, the rider should remain calm, quietly reassure the horse, and use his legs firmly but not harshly to insist that the horse moves. The horse should, ideally, move forward, but, in his fright, he may plunge in any direction to get away from the source of his fear. Since the rider's main concern will be to keep the horse on his feet, not to give him a dressage lesson, he should concentrate on sitting still and deep in the saddle, and allow the horse all the rein he needs until he regains his mental and physical equilibrium.

CURRENT AND DEPTH Both factors can vary drastically, especially in the sort of river mentioned above. It is not unusual for depth to vary from knee-deep to quite definitely too deep over a small area, with a consequent variation in current. Such waterways often have definite 'safe crossings', and it is prudent to follow someone who knows them. Failing this, they should be forded with considerable caution, and it is worth noting that in fast-flowing water, it is usually easier to see the river bed a few metres ahead than that portion which is under your feet.

OTHER HORSES Notwithstanding the advice to follow some-one with local knowledge, it is important not to follow anyone too closely through water, since, if there is a problem in front of you, your horse may be upset or impeded, or even tread on a fallen rider. I recall an instance of a rider suffering total immersion because the horse in front stopped abruptly in midstream, and her own mount lost his footing attempting evasive action. Although this may sound funny, it is a lot funnier if it happens to someone else, especially a long way from home on a cold spring day, and such a situation is, of course, potentially very dangerous.

5

Riding on Bad Ground

Bad ground is, to some extent, an intrinsic hazard of riding cross-country, and it is important to know how to cope with adverse ground conditions, since one can wait for ever for perfect going. There are, however, extreme conditions when the rider who has regard for his horse's (and his own) well-being will not knowingly risk riding, or, if conditions are localised, he will take pains to avoid them. In some instances, bad ground may occur in isolated pockets, due to variation in soil and terrain. When taking part in competitions, it is important to note such areas during course-walking, especially where they are on a potential line of approach to a jump, but also in any instance where they could interfere with the horse's action or progress.

There are three main categories of bad ground; hard, slippery and heavy. They have various causes (sometimes inter-related), and their effect will vary according to actual severity, and the conformation, temperament and training of the horse, and how he is ridden. Before studying them in detail, it should be remembered that it is the horse who has actually to handle these conditions, and the rider's role should be to provide assistance and encouragement, while remaining sensitive to his mount's efforts and needs where balance is concerned.

Hard Ground

Although there are some horses who seem impervious to the problems of moving on hard ground others, especially those with thin soles or conformation faults which accentuate jarring, hate it. No horse will actually benefit from prolonged work at the faster gaits on a hard surface, while jumping on such ground involves a considerable risk of concussive injuries. Hard rutted ('poached') ground is a wicked surface, as is a hard-beaten path through which tree roots protrude, and chalk uplands can, in summer, dry to the consistency of iron. Hard level ground covered by short, slick grass can produce a very slippery surface, although similar ground covered by long, coarse grass can provide quite reasonable going.

If the ground is very hard, the question of whether to risk the horse must be asked and, if he has any history of leg trouble, the answer must be no. If circumstances are such that a decision is made to 'chance it', the rider must be extra sensitive to the horse's reaction: a horse 'feeling' the ground will shorten his stride and move with less zest than usual, and will also tend to 'cat jump', trying to get close to the fences and jumping them gingerly. If he exhibits these tendencies, and the rider believes that ground conditions are not going to change during the course of the day, it may be wise to retire before any lasting damage is done.

If the hard ground is confined to a small area, the horse should be allowed to proceed at his own speed, which will almost certainly be rather slower than his normal 'cruising speed'. Since the horse will not be enjoying jumping, it will be necessary to give firm aids at the fences, but the rider should not expect him to lengthen into jumps, and should bear in mind that combinations will probably ride rather 'longer' than anticipated when walking the course.

Slippery Ground

We have seen one example of how a hard surface may be slippery as well, and this association continues wherever there is a thin layer of wet soil over rock or gravel, or where the top few millimetres of chalk have been softened by rain. Other slippery surfaces include loose scree on slopes, moss-covered boulders and some types of mud. However, the greatest potential danger is probably represented by frost and ice. While it is highly unlikely that any form of cross-country sport would continue in conditions of severe frost, there are times when organisers and participants believe, with some justification, that early frost and ice will clear in time for a planned event to go ahead. In such circumstances, it is quite possible that a rider will risk starting out while conditions are still rather poor, and he may, in fact, find himself participating in his chosen sport before there has been as much improvement as hoped for. Such occasions call for the exercising of commonsense, and the rider should, if in any doubt, allow caution to override the disappointment of withdrawing from an eagerly-awaited event. Should he decide to proceed, there are some areas where particular care is called for.

ROADS Metalled surfaces are extremely dangerous when coverered with frost, and worse still if there are patches of black ice. Whether hacking to an event, or crossing roads in the course of participation, great caution is the order of the day, and the only sensible gait is walk. Even then, the horse should be allowed to make steady progress, and not pressed into hurrying or lengthening his stride. If he cannot proceed at his chosen speed without slipping, the rider should dismount carefully, and lead him in hand on a good length of rein, thus making progress easier and safer for both partners.

HEDGES AND WALLS Frost and ice can remain in the areas shaded by such obstacles long after it has thawed elsewhere, making for a treacherous landing if jumping. Where fences of this type occur on a course, the organisers should be aware of the potential problem, and may be able to take preventative action such as spreading thick layers of straw if freezing conditions are anticipated. Failing this, affected obstacles should be left out of the course.

Where there is a likelihood of meeting such fences and conditions whilst crossing natural terrain, it is best to avoid jumping 'blind'. At all times when there is an element of frost in the ground the rider should concentrate on sitting still, applying the aids gently and in good time, and generally going steady, especially on hills and round bends. He should also ride with as light a hold of the reins as practical, and be prepared to slip them instantly if the horse loses his footing. These remarks also apply to riding on ground made slippery by other causes, although the degree of caution necessary will be determined by intelligent assessment of actual conditions. Jumping on slippery ground obviously calls for a good deal of discretion, but, where it is really necessary, it is best to approach fences quite slowly on a fairly short stride, and just allow the horse to 'pop' over.

Heavy Ground

Moving through heavy, sticky, going is obviously tiring for any horse, and, if a horse is not very fit, or has tired, there is a considerable risk of tendon strain.

Conformation has a significant impact upon a horse's ability to 'handle the mud', and, whereas some animals keep their rhythm and action surprisingly well in such ground, others really wallow in it. The rider can help in all cases by sitting quietly, retaining a light, but definite, rein contact, and keeping his legs firmly 'on' to encourage the horse to keep moving forwards. Some horses, disliking the going, will attempt to get through it as fast as possible, and plunge forward, losing their action further. If they can be dissuaded from so doing, and 'held together' with subtle support from the reins, then so much the better, but the rider must use his discretion; there is no point in starting a 'wrestling match', which will merely compound the problem. Jumping out of this ground requires considerable extra effort from the horse, and the rider must, therefore, concentrate upon generating and maintaining impulsion on the approach, and giving a good strong aid on take-off. The rider on a 'gassy' horse, who finds his mount somewhat anchored and subdued by the ground conditions, should not become complacent and make the mistake of underriding: the horse will need all the help and encouragement he can provide.

It is a bad principle, when jumping from heavy going, to ask for, or expect, the horse to 'stand off'. It will be much easier for him to get in a little close, and the rider who is over-exuberant in 'going for a long one' may find himself going alone, even if his horse is normally bold and keen. Since stride length and athleticism are both affected by these conditions, it should be borne in mind that combinations are going to ride 'longer' than normal.

With jumping out of heavy ground being generally difficult, the thinking rider will always be looking for ways to avoid doing so, seeking approaches with better going. In the hunting field, there may be various routes and options, and, in competition, astute course-walking can pay dividends. It is amazing how many competitors will aim for the same point of every jump, regardless of the fact that preceding horses have dug a deep, sticky trench along the same route. This is a circumstance which can be foreseen unless conditions change very suddenly, and, at many fences, a perfectly acceptable approach just a metre or so to one side of the expected 'popular' line can provide much sounder going. Round a whole course, the use of a little forethought and imagination can avoid many potential trouble-spots, and conserve the horse's energy for the occasions when the bad ground is unavoidable.

Other Abnormal Ground Conditions

Although most 'bad' ground can be broadly categorised under one of the headings above, there are some conditions which are rather different. These are worth examining briefly.

PLOUGH   This would generally be considered as heavy ground, but may actually vary immensely in respect of soil and furrow type. Some light soils, ploughed with shallow furrows, can provide a quite acceptable riding surface, whereas heavy, wet clay, furrowed deeply, can be considered uncrossable for normal purposes.

Plough is most commonly met out hunting, although some hunter trials (and a few point-to-points) still incorporate a ploughed field. Most fields under plough have a headland – a strip of untouched land around their perimeter – and it often makes sense to stick to this, both to avoid any possibility of riding over newly-sown crops, and to make things easier for the horse. If, however, it is necessary, and permissible, to cross the plough, this is best achieved by pursuing a course diagonal to the furrows.

ROCKY MOORLAND   Many moorland areas have stretches of basically good turf interspersed with outcrops of bedrock. It may be necessary to ride over such areas at some speed (for example, when hunting) and, while large rocks must obviously be avoided, it may be practically impossible to prevent the horse from stepping on a few smaller pieces. There are several points to bear in mind in such circumstances (and these are also applicable to riding through woodland where no path exists):

1) Whilst reasonable care must be taken, extraordinary efforts to pick a route will not only result in unduly slow progress, but are also likely to cause a collision with another rider who is adopting a more direct approach.
2) Even if travelling at some speed, the horse must be kept under control and attentive to the aids. Any intended changes of direction should be signalled to him decisively and in good time, to prevent sudden swerving, and especially the swerving of horse and rider in opposite directions.
3) The rider must be prepared to slip the reins should the horse stumble or slip.

Since most of these rocky outcrops have been weathered for a very long time, they cause very little damage to horses compared, for instance, to flints. However, a horse can still jar or bruise himself, and the rider should be sensitive to any sensation of his horse going short or uneven. If this happens, it may very well be a minor affair, causing the horse to go 'ouch' for a moment until the discomfort passes. If, however, lameness is marked or persists, then it will be necessary to dismount and investigate.

SNOW Fresh, powdery snow a few centimetres deep is quite rideable, although it is helpful to grease the soles of the horses' feet, to prevent compaction and 'balling'. The main hazard of such snow lies in what may be concealed beneath it in the form of roots, stumps, wire, etc. For this reason, open areas whose geography is well known are safer than paths through trees and areas near gateways. If the snow becomes frozen hard, or lies thinly over hard ground, then it should be treated with great caution, as with ice.

BOGS Some parts of the country contain bogs, which are to be studiously avoided, since galloping headlong into one may have consequences more dire than just getting muddy breeches. Since most cross-country activities are pursued along a defined course, it is probable that hunting is the only sport upon which bogs may impinge. Dangerous areas will be known to locals so it is sensible, if hunting a strange country, to take notice of any wide detours made by the rest of the field.

If, however, you find yourself alone in such an area, it is best to proceed with caution. Should you find the horse sinking over his fetlocks in sucking, smelly going, you should retrace your steps forthwith and head for higher, firmer ground. Even though the area may be just a harmless patch of wet land, plunging on in the hope that the going may improve is an unnecessary risk.

GENERAL PRECAUTIONS IN BAD GROUND Greasing the soles of the horse's feet prior to riding in snow or icy conditions has already been mentioned, and there are other precautions which can be taken when riding on bad ground; for example, fitting studs to the shoes (which need specially threaded holes for the purpose), and fitting over-reach boots (which protect the heels of the forefeet from being cut by the hind shoes). While such measures are sensible, they should be considered supplementary to, and not as substitutes for, careful and considerate riding.

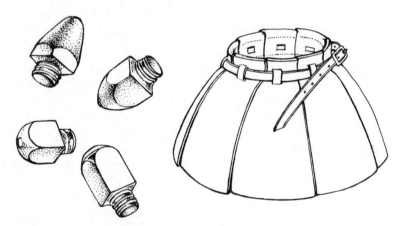

Studs and overreach boots

6

Intelligent Riding

No matter how technically proficient a rider may be, he will always risk being 'caught out' across country if he does not ride with his brain fully engaged. This is where rider 'cleverness', mentioned earlier, comes into play, and it is an essential hallmark of all good cross-country riders, regardless of their chosen sport.

Two major problems for inexperienced riders are lack of forward planning and lack of quick reaction, and observation suggests that these cause as much difficulty overall as does technically incorrect riding. The problems are, to some extent, a product of inexperience itself, but I feel that they are fostered by a general tendency for many instructors to concentrate exclusively upon technique, and by an insufficiently enquiring attitude on the part of many riders. I would, therefore, encourage the reader to place some emphasis upon the importance of thinking as an integral part of riding cross-country. There are three main areas where this is important.

Pre-planning

This includes anything relevant to the proposed ride: ensuring that the horse is fit and well, checking tack and protective clothing, leaving in good time to get to the venue without rushing, familiarising yourself with rules, etc. The crucially important aspect of pre-planning for competition riding is, of course, to walk the course thoroughly, since a wrong route or 'uninformed' refusal can negate the purpose of all other planning.

Current Awareness

I am using this phrase to convey the idea of the rider's being fully aware of what is happening beneath and around him at any particular moment. Although it is desirable to have the horse 'cruising' as much as possible across country, this does not mean that the rider can become a mere passenger; he must be constantly aware of how his horse is going, and making any adjustments necessary. If, for instance, he senses that the horse is about to quicken or slow down contrary to his own requirements, he must remedy the situation before it arises, although he must also be sensitive to underlying causes, especially those such as tiredness or lameness, which affect the horse's welfare. He must also have a good idea of how alert the horse is, and how readily and positively he is prepared to respond to direction from the saddle.

When riding in company, it is very important to know what other horses and riders are doing, in order to avoid being bumped, sandwiched or unsighted at a jump, or doing something similar to someone else. This is especially important in team or pairs hunter trials, where it may be desirable to be in close formation, but where you will not earn the undying admiration of team members by carrying them out at a fence, or jumping on top of them!

Looking Ahead

There are two aspects of this; a partly-physical and a purely mental one.

THE 'PHYSICAL' ASPECT It is obvious that, when crossing unfamiliar country, the more notice you get of any changes of terrain or imminent obstacles, the better you can prepare for them. However, even when competing on a course you have walked thoroughly, it is still most important to look ahead: a rider in front of you may be having difficulties which will entail your passing him, and members of the public, or other competitors may be walking the course without due regard to their safety and your clear passage. (To digress a little, if you are walking a course while a class is in progress, *do* glance behind you at regular intervals. If a rider is anywhere in the vicinity, move well out of any possible line to the fence, turn to face the oncoming rider, and stand still. Should you be on a narrow track, make as much room as possible – do not expect the rider to go crashing through the undergrowth to avoid you. Also, avoid course-walking with a dog in tow, especially one without a lead.)

THE MENTAL ASPECT Looking ahead concerns assessing how the horse is likely to cope with forthcoming obstacles in the light of those already jumped, and how he is going at present. It is unwise to make over-concrete assumptions (especially pessimistic ones) on this basis, but the knowledge can still be put to one's own practical advantage. For instance, if the horse has shown a marked aversion to a particular fence, and a similar one features further on, it may make sense to decide to abandon an approach originally envisaged in favour of whatever eventually proved successful in overcoming the problem. This is not the same thing as indecision; providing one's mind is made up in good time, and the 'new' approach is ridden decisively, it is a positive attempt to gain a desired result. Also, of course, I am not suggesting that the rider should be continually changing his mind as he proceeds round the course; most of the time the knowledge gained will merely be extra 'input' which he could only have guessed at when course-walking, but it should certainly prove a help rather than a hindrance.

Finally, on the topic of intelligent riding, it can be good practice to do some intelligent spectating, watching competitors at various levels, and asking oneself a lot of questions: 'How would I jump that?'; 'Why did that rider approach in that manner?'; 'Was that clever or lucky?', etc. If it is possible to spectate with a rider of considerable practical experience, this process can be even more informative. It is quite likely that the complete and correct answers to a number of the questions raised will never be known, but it is the stimulation of the thought processes which is valuable.

7

Competition Riding

Background

The cross-country jumping competitions with which this book concerns itself are hunter trials and the cross-country phase of horse trials (specifically one day events). Although these sports have somewhat different origins, it is probably fair to say that they have grown closer together over the years, with horse trials having an increasing effect upon hunter trials.

Hunter trials were, originally, very much 'fun' affairs, organised by individual hunts around the start and finish of the hunting season. Whereas the old time point-to-points were designed so that members could race their hunters, the purpose of the trials was to establish how well the horses could perform in a hunting environment. The trials took place across a typical piece of the local 'country', with the obstacles being virtually all natural. Therefore, in some areas the jumps would be mainly stone walls, in others, mainly hedges, or post-and-rails, or whatever was the popular local method of enclosure. Riders all wore full hunting dress, and the most common method of judging was to decide what would represent a 'fair hunting pace' for the course, and award the prize to the contestant who did the best round nearest to this time. Although the concept of a 'clear round' was recognised, style would sometimes also be taken into consideration.

The format of hunter trials did not, in fact, vary much until the fairly recent growth in popularity of horse trials in general and one day events in particular. Horse trials originated from a military background: there was, around the start of this century, a form of assessment of military horses in France, which involved testing jumping and galloping ability, qualities of endurance, and the level of schooling. This captured the imagination of military personnel who already had interests in equestrian sport, and the 'Militaire' soon became a sport in its own right: an embryonic 'Three Day Event'. With increasing civilian interest, mainly from amongst hunting people, the sport developed and spread rapidly, and the rules and format for horse trials were established. Since the 'Militaire' influence remained strong, and since most participants were well-connected owner-riders, all the early horse trials remained three day affairs, and the less demanding one day events, held over much shorter courses and to a simpler format, were established quite a while later.

Within the last 25 years or so, however, one day events have enjoyed rapidly-increasing support. They give the competitor an opportunity to participate in the three disciplines of dressage, show-jumping and cross-country on the same day and may, at club level, be organised so that relatively inexperienced riders can participate. Indeed, even the courses for official B.H.S. novice events (which are nowadays compulsory 'first steps' even for potential three day event horses and riders) are within the compass of the experienced 'club' rider on a 'good hunter' type of horse.

Because of the immense popularity of major horse trials as a spectator sport, however, their increasingly intricate and inventive fence design has had an influence at all levels, and many local courses now boast miniature versions of famous obstacles. These local courses are often on land belonging to a riding club or school, and are frequently used for hunter trials as well as for one day events, the former being easier to organise, and nearly as lucrative as the latter. At a more exalted level, many horse trials riders have taken to using open hunter trials as schooling grounds for young horses, or outings for those retired from major competition, and this seems to have further encouraged a departure from the original format.

The main influences of horse trials on hunter trials have, then, been in these areas:

OBSTACLES   Many hunter trial obstacles are now 'artificial', and there is a consequential increase in the number of 'island' fences (those built in isolation to any existing form of enclosure, specifically as competition jumps).

DRESS It is becoming increasingly rare to find hunter trials whose rules specify the wearing of hunting dress, and many now stipulate that skull caps must be worn.

PENALTIES Most hunter trials now make extensive use of the rules and penalties laid down in the British Horse Society's publication *Rules For Official Horse Trials*.

Because of these influences, we shall consider many of the rules and practises of the cross-country phase of horse trials on the understanding that they will normally apply to hunter trials as well. This does not, however, mean that the sports have become indistinguishable – some more traditional hunter trials have regulations and formats which have never been part of horse trials – and readers are advised to read schedules for *all* cross-country jumping competitions carefully, and to clarify any queries with the show secretary before competing.

Rules

The rules examined below are extracted from the British Horse Society's *Rules For Official Horse Trials*, as applicable to novice one day events. The British Horse Society also publish the *Riding Club Rule Book*, which contains a version of horse trials rules adapted a little to suit the requirements of club-level competition. There are some minor technical differences between the two, but they mainly concern characteristics of the course, and the rider who adheres to the *Horse Trials* rules is most unlikely to fall foul of the *Riding Club* ones. Both sets of rules are readily available, either direct from the B.H.S. at Kenilworth, Warwickshire, or from riding club secretaries, or specialist equestrian bookshops. They are well-worth studying in detail, since schedules for most competitions will merely state 'to be judged in accordance with B.H.S. rules for Horse Trials', and then give any exceptions.

Incidentally, although rules for the show-jumping phase of one day events are not dealt with below, competitors would be advised to familiarise themselves with the penalties for this discipline, which are at variance from those normally applied in pure show-jumping competitions.

Let us, then, examine the more fundamental rules, and the effect which their observance has upon the competitor. (Note the B.H.S. rules give metric measurements only.)

Time

The time/speed element affects virtually all cross-country jumping competitions in one form or another. In the cross-country phase of horse trials, there is a system of time penalties, which is based upon a pre-set optimum time. In B.H.S. novice one day events, the optimum time is calculated by dividing the length of the course in metres by a speed of 525m per minute. So, for example, a course 1680m in length would have an optimum time of $^{1680}/_{525} = 3\frac{1}{5}$th minutes, or 3 minutes 12 seconds.

While there is no advantage to be gained by going faster than the optimum speed, going slower incurs time penalties; one penalty for each commenced period of three seconds by which the optimum time is exceeded. Furthermore, there is also a time limit, which will be twice the optimum time. Failure to complete the course within the time limit incurs elimination, although it also suggests that the horse and rider have met with such trouble en route as to make this somewhat academic. In local and club competitions, the optimum time may well be calculated on the basis of a slower speed than 525m per minute, and the time penalties may also be more 'generous', but the basic concept is almost certain to be the same. There should be a plan of the course on display outside the secretary's tent, and this should give details of course length, optimum time, and the basis upon which time penalties are to be applied.

BOGEY TIME The system of time penalties, as such, is not normally applied in hunter trials, but they are often judged on 'bogey time', which has some similarities, and may give rise to initial confusion. The 'bogey time' for a course is that which the competition organisers feel represents a good, sensible pace at which to ride it (traditionally, the 'fair hunting pace'), and the winner is the rider who can complete a clear round nearest to the 'bogey'. Under this system, therefore, being faster than the 'bogey' is effectively 'penalised' to the same extent as being slower, although, in the event of a tie, one may be favoured over the other.

'Bogey times' are frequently employed for novice classes, the idea being that they discourage riders from trying to go too fast. For the same reason, although the time may be announced in advance, it is more usual for it to be kept secret until after the class, so that competitors are encouraged to ride at an even speed, and do not, for example, crash into trees whilst attempting to read their watches.

The other main method of timing hunter trials is on the basis of 'fastest clear round wins'. This is the most common form of judging for 'Open' classes, and is also used extensively for pairs and team events. (Incidentally, in the sport of Team Chasing, the criterion is usually 'fastest completed round wins', falls, refusals and all.)

Until you have gained a reasonable amount of competition experience, and have developed a good partnership with the horse, you would be wise not to pay too much attention to time, however it may influence the classes you enter.

In a local level one day event, providing reasonable progress is maintained, it is unlikely that many time penalties will be incurred, and they will almost certainly total fewer than those penalties which would result from a single run-out caused by a failed attempt to 'save time'.

Under the 'bogey time' system (especially where the time is kept 'secret'), one clear round has pretty much as good a chance of winning as another, and it is pointless to do anything other than go at a speed which suits yourself and your horse. With regard to classes judged on the 'fastest clear' basis, there is no harm entering them if they are convenient to attend and run over a good course, but the venture should be regarded as primarily for experience. This format inevitably attracts a number of experienced riders on fast horses, and the novice on a hired 'patent safety' cannot hope to compete, and will probably jeopardise his chances of a good clear round if he attempts to do so. The main drawback for the inexperienced rider participating in 'speed' classes is, however, the possibility of other riders wishing to overtake, which can affect both the concentration and the fluency of a round.

Course Markings and Signs _____

The essential elements of the course will be marked by red and white flags, and the rider *must* pass to the left of all red flags, and to the right of all white ones. These flags will be used to indicate the start and finish lines, and all obstacles which form part of the course, but may also appear either singly or in pairs at other key points, in which case they must still be respected. It is most important that the position of all such flags is noted when walking the course, since passing the wrong side of one constitutes an error of course which, if not corrected, will incur elimination. In addition to the red and white flags, there may also be direction markers on the course. At 'official' competitions, these will be yellow arrows, but at minor events they may well be cardboard pointers pinned to trees. In either instance, such markers are for information only, and there is no obligation to pass them to one side or the other, or even to go near them.

Class indicators are coloured number boards used where several classes are held over courses which include some common obstacles. The B.H.S. rules stipulate an official colour scheme to indicate specific classes, but, at many local shows, the organisers will use whatever they possess, or whatever takes their fancy. Therefore, it is important to study the course plan before walking the course, in order to ensure that you will be assessing the correct obstacles. Do not assume that the official colour scheme is being used, or that it is the same as for the last competition you entered. Once walking the course, make sure that you do not omit any fences in your class; check the sequence of numbers on the indicator boards. Also, where different parts of an obstacle are used for different classes, make certain that you *know* which portion you are permitted, or obliged, to jump.

The other signs with which riders should be familiar are the emergency flags. These are used by fence stewards to summon assistance, and the stipulated colours are red for the doctor, blue for the vet, and white for fence repairs. If it becomes necessary to stop a competitor, all three will be waved together, and, in such circumstances, it is *essential* to circle away from the fence and come to a halt; there may be an injured horse or rider on the landing side. Once the signal is given, the rider's time will be 'frozen', and timing will re-start once the course is clear, and an indication has been given to continue. Should you be held up in this manner, you should not allow the horse to 'go to sleep', nor should you insist upon his standing still. The best procedure is to walk and trot around, circling on each rein and riding a few transitions; this should keep the horse's attention without allowing him to fret and 'boil over'. It is normal practice for the fence steward to give some notice that the way will shortly be clear, and he is likely to tell the competitor that he may re-start in his own time, and that the clock will be started as a certain point is passed. Therefore, although you should not dither around once the 'all clear' is given, there is no need to panic, and it makes sense to take a couple of seconds to ensure that you have the horse's full attention before proceeding.

Penalties at Jumps

The standard penalties are:

1st refusal, run-out, or circle at an obstacle	20 penalties
2nd refusal, run-out, or circle at the same obstacle	40 penalties
3rd refusal, run-out, or circle at the same obstacle	Elimination
Fall of horse and/or rider at an obstacle	60 penalties

These penalties only apply if, in the opinion of the fence judge, they result from an attempt to negotiate a numbered obstacle. Falls on the flat, if occurring in isolation from a numbered jump, will not be penalised, neither will problems directly connected to an attempt to negotiate an 'optional' element. It should be noted that the former point is at variance with show-jumping rules (including those for the show-jumping phase of a one day event), and another difference is the position regarding the cumulative effect of refusals/run-outs, since, in show-jumping, a total of three refusals/disobediences *during the entire course* will incur elimination. Although the penalties listed may not be applied in some hunter trial classes judged purely on speed, they are applicable to most hunter trials and all one day events. It is, therefore, worth looking at the definitions of those actions which will incur penalties.

REFUSAL   A full stop in front of an obstacle is considered to constitute a refusal. A momentary pause, followed by a standing jump, will not be penalised, but a prolonged or established halt will be. The horse may hesitate and move sideways prior to a standing jump without penalty, but if any backward movement (even a single step) is discerned, then the horse is deemed to have refused. On this basis, as soon as a rider senses any backward movement, he should 'cut his losses' and re-present the horse, since fiddling around in front of the obstacle may well result in clocking up three pointless refusals, or even result in elimination for 'showing' the horse the fence.

Incidentally, if the horse 'naps' (refuses to move forward) on the flat, this is not penalised as for a refusal in cross-country competitions, although it is in show-jumping.

RUN-OUT   A horse is considered to have run-out if he avoids the obstacle and runs past the marker flag to one side or the other.

CIRCLE   A horse is considered to have circled if he crosses his original track while negotiating or attempting to negotiate an obstacle. This rule seems to have been designed to prevent the rider on a bad stride, or otherwise in trouble, from aborting his approach and having another go with impunity. However, it can prove a 'catch' for the rider who exercises insufficient control at combination obstacles (as we shall see in due course), and it is worthwhile adopting an attitude of 'think before circling'.

Notwithstanding this desire for caution, it is a misconception that completing a circle by crossing one's original track when re-presenting the horse after a penalised problem will incur further penalties. This is not the case, which is just as well considering that, in some situations, it may be impossible to avoid doing so.

FALL   A rider is considered to have fallen when he is separated from his horse in such a manner that he has to remount or vault back into the saddle.

A horse is considered to have fallen when his shoulder and quarters have either both touched the ground, or have touched the obstacle and the ground between them. While it is obviously possible for the rider only to fall, it is also technically possible for the horse only to fall. However, whether one, the other, or both end up on the ground, only one set of 60 penalties in incurred, providing the fall(s) results from a single incident.

Rules for Multiple Obstacles

Where several obstacles are situated close together, the course-designer's decision as to whether they constitute separate obstacles or one combination ('multiple') has a crucial bearing upon the application of penalties.

If they are considered to be separate obstacles, they will be numbered as such (8, 9, 10, etc.), and the rules and penalties already examined will apply. If, however, they are considered to be elements of one obstacle, only the first element will be numbered, and each will be marked with a letter (8A, B, C, etc.). All elements will still be marked with red and white flags.

In the case of combinations and multiples, the rules and penalties will be rather different from those applied to 'single' fences:

1) A competitor is only allowed a total of two refusals/run-outs/circles in negotiating the entire obstacle; he is not allowed two at each element.
2) Any circle between elements is penalised. (If the elements were numbered as separate obstacles, and a circle was not considered to be a result of attempting to negotiate an obstacle, there would be no penalty.)
3) If a competitor has a refusal or run-out at any part of the obstacle, he has the choice of retaking either that particular element, or the entire obstacle. This rule is at variance with the rule for show-jumping, whereby, in the case of a refusal/run-out at a latter element of a combination, it is compulsory to re-take the entire obstacle. It is also the exception to the general rule for the cross-country phase of horse trials under which re-taking an obstacle already jumped incurs elimination. The reason for this, however, is that, since the obstacle in question consists of several elements, it is not deemed to have been jumped until all the elements have been negotiated.

It is a good idea to ensure that you are fully conversant with these rules, so that you do not make a wrong decision in the heat of the moment.

Some applications of penalties in cross-country competitions

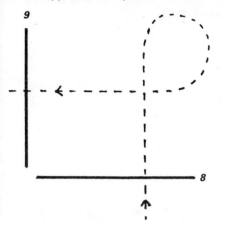

1) *Horse not presented at jump prior to circle. No penalty*

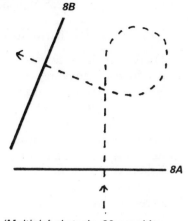

2) *'Multiple' obstacle. 20 penalties for any circle*

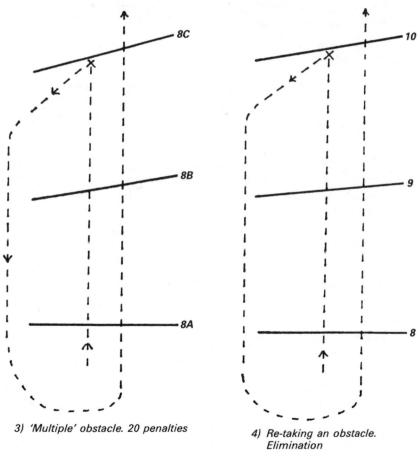

3) *'Multiple' obstacle. 20 penalties*

4) *Re-taking an obstacle. Elimination*

Causes of Elimination

There are a number of reasons why a competitor may be eliminated – they all, of course, come down to breaking rules. Some of the more common reasons have already been mentioned in passing, for example:

Third refusal/run-out/circle at the same obstacle.

Error of course not rectified.

Retaking obstacle already jumped.

Taking obstacles in the wrong order (which relates to the above two reasons).

Exceeding the time limit. (This may not apply in some hunter trials.)

There are, however, various other actions or omissions which will result in elimination, and it is important to be aware of them, so that a moment's ignorance does not spoil the day.

FAILING TO RETURN AFTER A FALSE START Don't allow the horse's enthusiasm to dictate in this matter.

FAILING TO START AFTER SIGNAL Within sixty seconds of the signal to do so you must start. Note that, in more formal one day events, you will be given a set time for starting in each phase, and the onus will be on you to be ready at that time. Although your number will be called a couple of minutes before your start time, no one is going to search the showground for you. Therefore, you can be eliminated not only for being physically unable to ride your horse through the start, but also for not being present within a minute of your allotted time. (By the same token, however, you are not obliged to start *before* your allotted time, even if requested to do so; the choice, in this instance, is yours.)

'SHOWING' THE HORSE AN OBSTACLE That is, letting him look at it in advance of attempting to jump it – or practising over it before the competition starts!

OUTSIDE ASSISTANCE It is not permitted to:
a) deliberately take a 'lead' from another competitor (this does not apply to team members in pairs or team hunter trials).
b) ask for directions or assistance from an outside agent, or receive them, even if they are unsolicited.

There are exceptions to b):
If a rider falls, it is permissible for another party to retrieve the horse, and assist the rider to remount.
If the rider has to dismount in order to adjust tack, he may be assisted in doing so, and also in remounting.
If spectacles, headgear or whip are dropped, they may be handed to the rider without his dismounting.

USING FORBIDDEN TACK   The rules of the B.H.S. forbid the use of blinkers, hoods, running and check reins (draw reins, market harboroughs, etc.) and standing martingales. These rules are adhered to at most non-B.H.S. competitions, although standing martingales may be permitted at some. Competitors may also be commanded to remove or adjust any tack which show officials consider unsuitable or ill-fitting, and failure to comply may result in elimination.

INCORRECT DRESS   The B.H.S. rules also stipulate military uniform, hunting dress or polo-neck sweater, breeches and boots for the cross-country phase of horse trials. In practice, a riding jacket with shirt and tie (or stock) will pass for 'hunting dress' and a striped rugby shirt or similar seems to have become a popular and accepted substitute for a polo-neck, even at 'official' competitions.

However, some hunter trials still specify 'hunting dress', and, although riders who turn up in cross-country colours are usually allowed to participate, they will be excluded from the prize list. It is, therefore, worth checking this point on the entry schedule. There has recently been much emphasis in the riding world upon safe headgear, and B.H.S. rules now make the wearing of a crash helmet (which may currently be taken to mean a hat to British Standard 4472) compulsory for the cross-country phase. A number of organisers have followed suit, and all will insist, at least, upon a 'correctly-fitting hard hat'. It is, incidentally, generally accepted nowadays that a crash helmet may constitute part of 'hunting dress'.

Therefore, although you may get away with a fairly liberal interpretation of 'correct dress' on most fronts, you will certainly not be allowed to compete at any reputable event without a reasonable degree of head protection.

OTHER In addition to these reasons for elimination, there are a few others which I hope never apply to readers. These are: injured or unfit rider, lame or unfit horse, cruelty to horse (including excessive/improper use of whip or spurs), improper schooling procedures and bad conduct.

Special Rules for Hunter Trials _____

PAIRS AND TEAM CLASSES Pairs and teams-of-three classes are quite popular at hunter trials, and are usually judged on speed, with the time of the last horse to cross the finish counting. In such classes, the standard jumping penalties may well be waived or modified, and it is important to know exactly what the rules are before starting. This type of competition is really more suitable for reasonably experienced riders on familiar horses, than for novices on hirelings. However, a 'school' round in a pairs class in the company of a helpful and experienced partner can be a valuable education for a novice, be he human or equine.

DRESSING FENCES It is quite common for teams and pairs classes to include some 'dressing' fences, which the riders are required to jump abreast, there being a set time penalty for failure to do so. In order to tackle a dressing fence safely and well, it is important to pre-arrange a 'marshalling point' some way before the obstacle so that the riders can group up and approach it in unison. It is obviously neither safe nor effective to have the leading rider checking back frantically, and the tail-ender coming in at a flat-out gallop, in an effort to arrive at the fence together. Furthermore, however much the team may wish to jump in perfect formation, the individual riders should give first priority to riding a good approach themselves, since a fall or refusal may cause more harm to both the individual concerned and the team effort than would a few 'dressing penalties'.

GATES Some more traditional hunter trials include a gate as an obstacle. This has to be opened, ridden through, and shut, and there is usually no penalty for dismounting. Jumping the gate, however, is not usually permitted, the idea being to simulate a gate met out hunting in circumstances where jumping would be impractical, and to test the handiness of horse and rider under such conditions.

In most cases, negotiating the gate merely adds to the competitor's time for the course, with an extra penalty being imposed for failure to do so. In some instances, however, the gate may form the start or finish of a 'timed section'.

TIMED SECTIONS These are incorporated into some hunter trials which are not judged primarily on speed, but where speed over a short section of the course is used as a deciding factor to find a winner. This idea seems to detract from the principle of making as smooth progress as possible across country, but it is not uncommon, and the competitor with serious intentions of trying to win such a class should make sure that he is fully conversant with the 'local rules'.

Procedures for Entering a Competition _____

Although these are really quite straightforward and logical, they are much more so when one is familiar with them. As I have never read a book on riding which explained how to enter a competition, it may be worth looking briefly at what is involved.

PRELIMINARIES Competitions are advertised in riding magazines, riding club newsletters, and on posters at stables. Details are laid out in 'schedules', which are obtainable from the show secretary. If applying for a schedule by post, remember to enclose a large stamped, addressed envelope and remember also to write 'schedule please' on its cover.

Once you have received the schedule, study the rules under which the competition is to be held, and the conditions of entry for each class, choosing the class(es) most suitable for you in terms of eligibility, height of jumps and probable starting times. With hunter trials, do not enter more than two classes in the day – it is unfair on the horse (and yourself). Furthermore, unless you have good reason to believe that you will be able to go early in one, and late in the other, avoid entering consecutive classes.

Once you have completed the entry form, be sure to post it, together with the entry fees, well before the closing date.

Sometimes late entries will be accepted if the class is not full, but there will usually be a late entry surcharge. Should you wish to make a late entry, it is in everybodys interest for you to telephone the organisers first.

When entering a one day event, you will usually see from the schedule that it is necessary to telephone the show secretary at a certain time and date in order to obtain your starting times. Do not neglect to do so, and endeavour, as far as possible, to telephone at the specified time. Should you be unable, after entering, to attend the competition, it is a matter of courtesy to inform the organisers. However, unless you are able to furnish a doctor's or vet's certificate, it is unlikely that your entry fee will be refunded.

ON THE DAY Ensure that you reach the venue in good time. On arrival, go to the secretary's tent, declare your entry, and collect your number cloth. You will usually have to pay a refundable deposit on this (normally £1 or £5), so make sure you have the money to hand. Check whether the classes are running to time; variations can have a considerable effect upon your planning, riding in, etc. At one day events, even if they are running an hour late, it may be prudent to present yourself to the stewards of each phase at the appointed time (if you *know* it is well behind time, it is not necessary to take the horse with you).

At hunter trials, it is not usual to be allocated a starting time. Normally, the starter's assistant will take declarations from about half an hour before the start of each class. This is done simply by writing competitors' numbers on a blackboard. The numbers will basically be listed in sequence of starting, but it is quite in order to say that you would like to go 'early', 'about thirtyeth', 'right at the end', or whatever, although you cannot expect to 'queue jump'. Although the onus will then be on you to check when your time is approaching, you will not normally be eliminated from a Hunter Trial if you are not around when it is your turn to start: you will just be dropped down the order. Nevertheless, it is easier for all concerned if you *are* ready to take your turn.

Semi-Competitive Sports

RIDE AND TIE This is a fairly recent development in equestrian sport, although it is based upon a centuries-old means of travel.

The principle of the sport is that two riders and one horse have to travel a set route either as quickly as possible or within defined time limits. The event begins with one person riding, and the other on foot, and, at certain points along the course, the rider dismounts and 'ties' (tethers) the horse, proceeding on foot whilst the other team member, on arrival at the tethering point, takes over riding.

Ride and tie has become very popular in the United States, where it is often organised on a seriously competitive basis. In Britain, however, it is still a comparative rarity, typically arranged at local level as a 'fun' event. The only national equestrian body which currently promotes ride and tie in Britain is the Arab Horse Society, which organises both serious and less serious competitions. These are being well supported, and the A.H.S. hope to pursue a continuing policy of expansion in this area. While the Arab breed is generally well-suited to the sport, A.H.S. competitions are open to all breeds, as is normally the case with events organised by other bodies.

Depending upon the level of competition, the total distance covered in a ride and tie may be from 12.8km (8 miles) to 41.6km (26 miles). While even the shorter distance requires a reasonable degree of fitness in horses and riders, the longer distances require serious preparation and, at all levels, there are veterinary checks en route to ensure the well-being of the horses. For the riders' part, although events should have medical assistance available in case of serious injury, competitors often address the fundamental problems of riding in running gear by applying padding to their saddles.

Although proper consideration of fitness is important, ride and tie does not, at the less serious levels, require a particularly fast or talented horse, and jumping is not usually a factor. Furthermore, the main requirements of the riders are that they are considerate horsemen, sufficiently competent to remain in balance and control when tired themselves. Since the sport also has the advantage of being relatively inexpensive, it is within the compass of many riders, and would be especially suitable for two like-minded people who share a horse.

Readers wishing to do so can obtain further details about ride and tie from the Show Secretary of the A.H.S.

OBSTACLE RIDES These have gained in popularity in recent years, and are normally organised with a view to benefiting charitable organisations. They usually take place in very pleasant surroundings, over extensive areas of land which is either in private ownership or administered by conservators, the National Trust, etc.

The ride is usually about 16 to 19km (10 to 12 miles) in length, although some may be as long as 32km (20 miles). There will be a number of flagged obstacles along the route, all of which are optional, although the rider will be sponsored on the basis of number of fences jumped. Entry fees are often a little lower than for a comparable competitive event, but it may be a condition of entry that the rider has been sponsored for a certain (fairly modest) sum.

Some rides contain a competitive element, for instance a 'pairs' class, with a prize for the pair who collect the most jumping points, time being the deciding factor in the case of equality. The competition has to be considered light-hearted, however, since regard for other riders, compulsory stops at marshalled road crossings, and the total distance involved make time, to some degree, reliant upon luck.

To ease administrative difficulties, jumping 'points' are usually awarded on a simpler basis than normal cross-country penalties. For instance, some fences may be divided into 'small' and 'large' categories, with five points being awarded for jumping a small fence, and ten points for a large one (jumping both sections of the same fence doesn't earn both sets of points). In the event of a refusal or fall, no points are earned for that obstacle.

Obstacle rides are attractive to a considerable cross-section of riders. Apart from the charitable connection, they can be a good schooling ground for both inexperienced riders and horses, since the competitive element is minimal, which gives some time for deliberation, and there is also the opportunity of introduction to the demands of travelling in company without the pressures imposed by hunting or mock hunting. They are also attractive, of course, to the rider who has no competitive aspirations but who enjoys crossing pleasant country at his own speed, jumping what he chooses.

8
Non-Competitive Sports

Foxhunting

Foxhunting fulfils two roles: it is an effective method of controlling the fox population without using the draconian methods of poison or introduced disease; and following hounds on horseback constitutes one of the oldest-established equestrian sports. Several other sports have their roots in foxhunting, and hunter trials and point-to-points owe their existence to it.

Although it has, in recent years, become misunderstood in some quarters (mainly in urban areas), and has suffered from the general erosion of the countryside, foxhunting continues to thrive and, for many of its adherents, following hounds is the epitome of cross-country riding. It may come as a surprise to learn that it is a sport within the compass of the 'ordinary' rider, both in terms of its demands on equestrian ability and, if done occasionally and selectively, the pocket. Certainly there are some very 'posh' hunts, which are, frankly, too expensive for most people; there are also those which require a lot of experience and a very good horse in order to be properly appreciated, but there are many which will provide a very enjoyable day without undue risk of physical or financial injury.

For the reader who has never been hunting, but has a general interest in doing so, the crucial questions will be: 'What actually goes on?'; and 'How would I fit in?' The long answer to the first question will not be fully discovered in a lifetime of participation, such is the variety of the sport, but the short answer is that hunting is what goes on, and the fundamental purpose of riding to hounds is to follow the progress of the hunt. Depending upon circumstances, this may mean galloping further than you have ever galloped in your life, or it may mean sitting at rest for some time watching a hound hunt; it may mean jumping thirty fences in as many minutes, or it may mean spending the whole day without leaving the ground. Most hunts will provide sport which involves a varied mixture between these extremes, but it is important to realise that hunting is not solely about galloping and jumping, and the rider who is exclusively interested in these aspects of equestrian sport would be advised to stick to competitive cross-country riding. Nonetheless, it is not uncommon for people who *think* that they only want to gallop and jump to find themselves increasingly fascinated by the other aspects of hunting.

To the question 'how would I fit in?' the answer is 'probably very well'. The idea of hunts populated exclusively by demented old colonels damning everyone in sight is no more than popular myth, and most hunts these days have a very democratic cross-section of followers whose common bond is enthusiasm for the sport. My own experience is that hunts extend a warm welcome to visitors and, whilst it is expected that the etiquette of the sport is observed, this just consists of a blend of common courtesy with actions and observances designed to assist the efficiency of the hunt.

BASIC RULES AND ETIQUETTE   There are many books which explain the lore, etiquette and traditions of the hunting field in great detail, and they make fascinating reading. However, all that is really required of the ordinary rider to hounds is that he avoids interfering with hounds or hunt staff in the course of their work, and that he behaves in a courteous and considerate manner. Observation of the following points should ensure that you do nothing to cause offence or disruption:

1) If intending to go to a meet as a visitor, it is courteous to telephone the hunt Secretary beforehand, to introduce yourself and ask permission. Although it is quite rare for 'fields' to be limited, there are occasions when this has to be done for practical reasons, and an enquiry can avoid embarrassment.

2) Arrive at the 'meet' in good time, seek out the hunt Secretary, introduce yourself and offer your 'cap' (day's subscription). Do not wait to be asked for it.

3) Never allow your horse to kick or trample hounds. The hunt staff will say 'hounds please' when they require room for the pack, and you should move well out of their path. In confined spaces, turn the horse's head toward hounds so that he can see them, and so that his hindlegs are kept well out of the way.

Turning the horse's head to face hounds

4) Don't ride around or chatter while hounds are 'drawing' (trying to find a fox).

5) Always make way for the Master and hunt staff, and obey any requests from them promptly.

6) Don't ride in pursuit of hounds until the Field Master has indicated that it is in order to do so, and don't ride in front of him unless he gives permission.

7) One of the Field Master's tasks is to ensure that hunt followers do not ride onto land where they have no permission to be, and it is therefore important that you do not 'take your own line' when on private property.

8) Thank anyone who opens a gate for you. Close unattended gates when you have passed through unless you know that there is someone following close behind. If another member of the field dismounts to open a gate do not gallop through and disappear; wait a few yards away until they have remounted.

9) Thank all drivers who make way for you on the road. Hunts and hunt followers do not have an automatic right of way.

10) If there is a queue at a jump, wait your turn. Do not barge, or allow your horse to cart you, in front of other people. If you have a refusal, get out of the way quickly, go to the back of the queue, and take a lead (although you must be reasonably close behind a lead, you should never jump right on the heels of the rider in front).

WELFARE OF HORSE AND RIDER These are commonsense points, but should not be overlooked in the excitement of the moment:

1) Don't ride faster than is necessary to keep in touch with the hunt.
2) Don't jump unnecessary fences.
3) Remember the basic techniques of cross-country riding; don't hurry the horse on bad or unlevel ground, and present him at all obstacles as well as circumstances permit.
4) When there is a check after a run, turn the horse's head into the breeze to assist him in recovering his breath.
5) Don't get involved in crowds in confined spaces, and keep well clear of horses with ribbons tied to their tails. (Red indicates a horse which may kick, and green indicates a young horse.)
6) In unfamiliar country, jump with caution. This does not mean that you should approach obstacles in a half-hearted fashion, but rather that you should, wherever possible, ensure that they are safe before taking them. This will usually mean taking them after several regular followers have negotiated them safely, but it may, at times, involve personal inspection.

    Fences with a 'blind' landing may have a big drop, a landing on a metalled road or other unsuitable surface, or even have farm machinery parked on the far side. Hedges in some areas may be reinforced with wire. Stone walls should not be jumped through a gap; the missing stones are frequently littered on the ground on one, or both, sides of the wall.
7) After the hunt, if hacking a tired horse home, remember that the idea is to bring him to his stable as dry and mentally settled as possible. Normally, most of the journey, and especially the last mile or so, should be made at walk, with the girth slackened slightly. It is, however, better to keep the horse walking forward into a light contact than to allow him to slop

along on a totally loose rein, since tired horses carelessly ridden can easily stumble and knock or strain themselves.

If it is very cold and wet, the horse may show a preference for periods of steady trot; as he will probably just be trying to prevent himself from getting chilled, this should be permitted as long as he keeps calm and does not start sweating. Discretion and commonsense are called for here, but you will be doing the horse no more service by bringing him home half-frozen than you would if bringing him home sweated up.

DRESS Many potential riders to hounds are very worried about what to wear; they conjure up memories of old hunting prints and assume that the garb depicted is still the norm. Although there is a great tradition of 'dress' in the hunting world, analysis of 'correct' clothing will show that it is extremely practical, the single exception being the top hat, which is becoming increasingly rare, and which is certainly not the only acceptable headgear!

There are many books on hunting which explain the traditions of dress, and what constitutes correct attire, and the reader who becomes an enthusiastic and regular follower of hounds will doubtless wish to kit himself out correctly in due course, since formal hunting dress provides greater comfort and protection than any substitute. For the time being, however, we shall concern ourselves with that which is generally acceptable, and which will not involve the average rider in significant extra expenditure. Nevertheless, before looking at individual items of clothing, it is important to remember that one hunts as a guest of, and by permission of, the hunt and local landowners, and it is a matter of courtesy to appear neat and tidy, even if the attire is not strictly 'correct' in all respects.

HEAD GEAR It is generally accepted that many people now wish to hunt in crash helmets, complete with harness, and it is much more sensible to do so than to borrow an ill-fitting bowler in an attempt to look 'correct'. However, if your usual cross-country 'colours' include a brightly-coloured cap silk, this should be replaced for the occasion by a black one.

Normal-pattern hard hats are traditionally worn by hunt staff and farmers, but have largely replaced the bowler as headwear for ordinary followers. They should, however, be black.

JACKET   Black is the norm for hunting and, although it will provide nowhere near the warmth and protection of a proper hunt coat, a show jacket will suffice. If you wear one in mid-winter, however, ensure that it is roomy enough to accommodate several layers underneath without splitting.

There is a form of hunt dress known as 'ratcatcher', traditionally worn for cubhunting (before the start of the season proper), and this consists of tweedy apparel. Therefore, in the absence of a black jacket, you may be able to base your dress around a tweed hacking jacket.

SHIRT   With a black jacket, a white, collar-less hunt shirt with stock is normal. If you do not possess a hunt shirt you can wear all sorts of things in lieu, provided you tie your stock cleverly. A normal shirt with black tie would be acceptable, but it is 'incorrect', and does look rather 'first-time-ish'.

With a tweed jacket, you can wear an appropriate pastel-shade hunt shirt and stock, or normal shirt and tweed tie.

BREECHES OR JODHPURS   Ordinary beige coloured stretch breeches or jodhpurs are perfectly acceptable, but be sure that they start the day clean. If you only possess coloured breeches, you will have to obtain something more traditional. The problem with stretch breeches is that they are nowhere near as warm as twill hunting breeches, so, in cold wet weather you would be well-advised to wear long-johns or footless tights underneath!

BOOTS   You must wear a proper pair of riding boots, both from the point of view of propriety and protection. Clean rubber boots will be acceptable and, in 'countries' where there is much scrambling about in wet places and fording of streams, many regular followers prefer them. Leather boots, however, look much smarter and, in most circumstances, are much more comfortable. I would suggest that they are a worthwhile investment for anyone riding regularly, whether they hunt or not. The drawback with wearing 'ratcatcher' is that you should really wear brown (tan) boots with it, and not many riders possess such footwear.

SPURS   Spurs are part of correct hunting dress. However, unless you are riding a horse you know well, on whom you habitually wear them, I would strongly advise you to refrain from putting them on 'for show'. You may well make a bigger exhibition of yourself than you bargained for!

WHIP   It is correct to carry a proper hunting whip with lash, and this can be a useful implement for dealing with gates. However, it is virtually useless for encouraging or disciplining a horse, and if your mount has a tendency to refuse at jumps, or kick out, it is in everyones interest for you to carry a normal whip.

GLOVES   Although there are conventions about correct gloves, the important thing when riding a keen horse on a cold wet day is to wear gloves which will assist you to hold the reins. Standard, leather-palmed riding gloves are pretty well essential in such conditions, and will offend even the most fastidious traditionalist much less than being ridden into by someone who is unable to control his horse. Incidentally, until you have tried to hold a keen horse with wet, slippery reins and numb fingers, you will not believe how impossible it is. A good pair of gloves as described above should be standard 'cross-country' wear, regardless of the specific sport involved.

WATERPROOFS   Although hunt staff and diehards never wear anything over their hunt coat, it is generally acceptable for ordinary hunt followers to wear a proper riding mac in bad weather. Some hunts will also countenance a respectable waxed cotton waterproof jacket, although it is probably true to say that they do not really like to see the field thus attired. A fluorescent pink anorak emblazoned with the name of your favourite rock band will not be appreciated. In the matter of waterproofs, it is best to take a lead from the regulars.

CHOOSING A HUNT AND HIRING A HORSE   The rider who wishes to hunt, and who owns or shares a horse stabled near an area which is hunted (a 'country'), may well decide to follow the local pack. In these circumstances he will readily be able to obtain information about the hunt, and be put in touch with the secretary by making enquiries amongst his riding acquaintances.

The rider who does not have regular access to a suitable horse will need to hire one and, although he too may wish to hunt locally, it is also possible that he may choose to take a short holiday in a preferred country in some other area. If this is the case, there are several lines of enquiry open to him. The best recommendation may well come from a friend who has already visited various hunts, and who can provide first-hand information about types of country, hiring yards, accommodation and costs. Failing this, *Baily's Hunting Directory*, published annually, gives detailed information regarding hunts nationwide. The weekly *Horse And Hound* also carries a summarised directory just before the start of each season (usually in late October), and, during the season, it carries brief weekly reports from various hunts, which give some insight into their countries and activities. Furthermore, *Horse And Hound* and some other riding magazines contain advertisements from hotels and stables which offer package hunting weekends.

If operating 'blind', it is a good idea to telephone the secretary of any hunt in which you are interested, and ask for details and advice. Such people are certain to know of the existence of reputable hiring yards and either they, or the stable proprietor, may be able to recommend local accommodation.

For the benefit of the reader whose experience of hiring horses consists of the occasional escorted hack, or going to shows at the hiring yard, it should be pointed out that hiring a hunter is a rather different business. In most hunting areas there will be several reputable yards which will provide horses suitable to their clients' requirements, and capable of giving a good day's hunting. The normal procedure is that the yard will provide boxing to the meet (if it is beyond hacking distance), and will pick you up afterwards, or else escort/direct you to the meet if it is local. For the duration of the hunt, however, it is up to you to look after yourself and the horse. Therefore, although people are usually very helpful in the event of any problems, there are some sensible precautions you should take:

1) You should be confident in your ability to ride a trained, but unfamiliar, horse both alone and in company at all gaits, and to ride safely on the public road.

2) If you have not hunted before, or have any qualms, tell the stable when you first approach them about hire. All good hire yards have at least one horse 'your granny could hunt' and this

will not be a 'slug' but (typically) a good-natured cob who knows and enjoys his job, and who is quite capable of looking after himself and his rider.

3) For obvious reasons, ensure that you *do* hire from a proper hunting yard with a good local reputation. Do not be tempted to go somewhere dubious in order to save a few pounds.

4) It is advisable to go out with at least one friend, preferably of greater experience than yourself, and sufficiently well-disposed toward you that, if he has to choose between following a good 'run' and stopping to pull you out of a manure heap he will (probably) choose the latter course. (You can increase your chances in this respect by ensuring that you are the one with the hip flask.)

5) If you do intend to go out alone for the first time, it is worth explaining to the proprietor of the yard or the hunt secretary that you are not familiar with the country, and asking if there is a regular follower who would be prepared to show you the ropes. The chances are that there will be someone pleased to do so, and their local knowledge may well save you a lot of unnecessary galloping about, and still get you to the right place in front of most of the field.

6) As a 'belt and braces' measure, it may be a good idea to carry a map of the locality, especially if the area is completely unknown to you.

CREATURE COMFORTS   Most hunts meet at 11.00 a.m., and, although the duration will vary, you can expect to be out for about five hours. It is, therefore, eminently sensible to have a good breakfast, and to take some sandwiches in your jacket pocket (although choosing when to eat them can be a nerve-wracking business).

Since hunting is fundamentally a winter sport, and tends to consist of periods in which one gets very hot, followed by periods of standing around, it makes good sense to wear plenty of clothing, and to err slightly on the side of too many layers, rather than too few.

If you do not normally ride for extended periods, it is worthwhile doing rather more than usual in the period leading up to a day's hunting, otherwise you may find yourself finishing the day very tired and sore. Incidentally, since unfamiliar saddles have a habit of removing the skin from the insides of one's knees, it is a good idea to protect these areas with large stiching plasters or strips of elasticated bandage. The reader who would prefer a rather gentler introduction in (hopefully) reasonable weather would be advised to start with a day's cubhunting. This takes place in the autumn, the cubs in question being virtually full-grown first year foxes. 'Cubbing' usually starts rather earlier in the morning, but is normally a 'half day' affair. Although it is less likely that you will experience a long 'run' when cubhunting, there is often plenty of activity, and it can provide a good introduction to the sport in many ways.

Mock Hunting

Mock hunting, like drag hunting, tends to take place in semi-rural areas and is designed to give participants the opportunity to have a good fast ride, and jump numerous fences along pre-determined routes, which often incorporate sections of existing hunter trial courses.

Mock hunts are organised by riding clubs, stables with a large regular clientele, or 'Mock Hunt' clubs, who concentrate upon this pursuit. 'Meets' are advertised as appropriate, although an association with the organising body is usually a requirement for participants. Payment is usually by 'cap' at the meet, but some riding clubs ask members for payment in advance. The accent in mock hunting is upon accommodating the 'ordinary' horse and rider, and obstacles are mainly less demanding than those encountered on drag hunts.

In mock hunts, all the roles of hunting are played by riders. One, who is the 'fox', departs from the meet and is given a couple of minutes to get clear before several other riders – the 'hounds' – go in pursuit. They are then followed by the 'field'. The theory is that the 'hounds' and field try to catch up with the 'fox', but, in practice, there is very little chance of this happening unless the 'fox' gets lost or falls off. The main purpose of the 'hounds' is that they are competent riders who know the area, and can give the field a lead in the right direction. One of the organisers also acts as Field Master, fulfilling a role similar to that of a Field Master in hunting proper, in keeping the field off land which is not to be ridden over. At intervals, there are pre-arranged 'checks' in order to give horses and riders a breather, allow stragglers to catch up, and generally re-organise before the next 'run'. Because of the fairly fast pace, and limitations of fitness of some horses (and riders), mock hunts usually last about two to three hours in total.

As a sport, mock hunting has some points to recommend it, and some drawbacks, and these are heightened by the organisation of the particular hunt. Some are very well organised, with interesting and varied obstacles, and attract fields of generally competent riders. Others are a shambles, with boring, ill-fenced terrain and riders careering around out of control, and generally getting in the way. As with most things, the majority fall somewhere between these extremes, and riders with past experience of a particular mock hunt can usually give one an idea of what to expect.

In general, the advantages of mock hunting are:

1) It can provide a useful introduction to the demands of crossing country in company, without the possible trauma of getting lost in unknown territory, and without the rider having to concern himself with some of the issues of hunting proper (heading the fox, trampling hounds, etc.).

2) Good mock hunts are very enjoyable in themselves.

The drawbacks are:

1) If the rider is insufficiently experienced, he may find the demands of jumping three or four abreast, and generally controlling an excited horse in company, rather daunting.

2) On the same basis, although a novice horse with an experienced rider, or a novice rider with an experienced horse, can both enjoy, and learn from, mock hunting, it is not the best pursuit for a novice combination.

3) Badly organised mock hunts are very tedious, and those where a significant proportion of the field is out of control resemble a dodgem ride more than anything else.

Dress for mock hunting is nominally 'hunting dress', but, in practice, normal boots, breeches, jacket and hard hat, with shirt and tie or stock, are worn by most participants.

9

Respecting the Horse

The cross-country rider is going to make considerable mental and physical demands upon his horse, and will inevitably, at times, rely upon him to make extraordinary efforts to get the partnership out of trouble, which will most probably be of the rider's making. He has, therefore, an obligation to the horse to avoid subjecting him to unnecessary stress, to be sensitive to any signs of lameness or discomfort, and to ride as well and as positively as possible at all times. It should be superfluous to add that the actual ownership of the horse has no bearing whatsoever upon these obligations. Although this is not a book on horsemastership, the subject is inseparable from these principles, and it is incumbent upon everyone who rides cross-country to familiarise themselves with the basics. Those fortunate enough to own a horse should, of course, go rather further into the subject.

When studying horsemastership in detail, areas for special consideration by the cross-country rider are:

Fitness and Soundness

A horse has to be at least reasonably fit in order to perform across country. It does not take an expert to form a general opinion of a horse's state of health and fitness, and all riders should learn to read the key signs. An unsound horse cannot readily be got fit, and should certainly not be ridden across country so, while a less experienced rider may not be able to discern a slight unlevelness of action, especially in a strange horse, it is most important to be able to feel, or see, obvious signs of lameness. Apart from the consideration of the horse's welfare, these points will be of personal interest to those hiring horses and expecting a good, trouble-free ride for their money.

If personally involved in getting a horse fit, remember that a gradual increase in steady, regular work is called for, along with a gradual increase in hard feed, up to a sensible ceiling for both. Overfeeding, and the untutored administration of laboratory-produced additives, are very dangerous for the horse (and possibly the rider). Variety in work and exercise will benefit the horse, but galloping an unfit horse will only put abnormal strain on limbs, lungs and heart, and too-frequent galloping of a fit horse will induce staleness and loss of condition.

Remember that there are no short-cuts to fitness, and attempting any will only create problems.

Training

Although this subject mainly concerns owners/sharers, it should be borne in mind that *all* riding will affect the horse's training for better or worse, and that bad riding tends to have a faster, and more marked, influence than does good riding.

Any horse is bound to perform better in any sphere if he has been correctly trained. The horse ridden in horse trials will, of course, have to do dressage tests, so his level of training on the flat will need to be rather higher than that of a horse ridden exclusively in non-competitive sports. Nevertheless, all horses will give a better ride if they have received correct basic schooling on the flat, and are given the occasional refresher session.

Good basics are of much greater value than indifferent 'fancy stuff', and the rider involved in schooling should concentrate on getting the horse moving freely forward onto the bit, and bending well on turns (indicating suppleness and balance). An ability and willingness to move away from the leg, and to rein back, can be of great practical advantage when dealing with gates and manoeuvering in confined spaces, but schooling in these movements should not be overdone.

With regard to schooling over jumps, it is most important to bear in mind that the purpose is to educate the horse and increase his confidence. If he is being introduced to a new type of obstacle, he should, initially, be introduced to the *principle* of it, over a small, easy version. Any refusal should be treated seriously – not by punishing the horse, but by assessing what it is about the obstacle that is causing him concern, and taking appropriate and sympathetic action. Persistent refusals during a schooling session are usually a sign that the rider has lost sight of what he is trying to achieve.

It is instructive to note that most leading horse trials riders school over surprisingly small fences at home. This is because they are not trying to prove points, but rather to boost the horse's confidence in his own ability, and the rider's judgement, to such a level that he will happily tackle any obstacle at which he is presented. Such confidence and trust are the cross-country rider's greatest assets, but retaining them is a heavy responsibility, which is why top riders never stop trying to improve their own standards and abilities. This is an example from which all riders can learn.

Tack and Equipment

No horse will go well in tack which is ill-fitting, uncomfortable or inappropriate, and he may suffer galling and soreness as a result of its use. All tack should, therefore, be clean, supple and a good fit, and new saddles, girths and bits should not be given their first outing on a lengthy or strenuous ride.

The rider can suffer from inappropriate saddlery in much the same way as the horse, but, in some circumstances, the results may be much more serious. Stirrup irons which are too large or too small can be very dangerous, as can any equipment in a poor state of repair. Saddles which do not fit the rider, or which are unsuited to the demands of riding cross-country, can have an adverse effect upon a rider's technique as well as his comfort, and reins which cannot be held properly in adverse conditions can cause problems for horse, rider, and other people. (My own strong preference is for rubber-gripped reins.)

In general, the best rule for tack is 'the simpler the better', and I have every sympathy with the B.H.S. prohibition of standing martingales and other gadgetry from use in horse trials. I would also advise the average rider to avoid using a double bridle across country, at least in jumping events. Although some horses go very well in a 'double' and its use by experienced riders is not uncommon, the two sets of reins can prove rather difficult to handle in moments of crisis, and it can, therefore, be a problem to retain the correct function of the bit and bridoon. The rider who does decide to use a double bridle across country should first be fully conversant with its correct application in other circumstances, and it should certainly not be fitted as a 'brake'.

As far as bitting in general is concerned, a fairly basic type of snaffle is usually best, and the rider who follows the principles outlined earlier in this book should be able to control most horses in such a bit. You should always be very reluctant to change to a more severe bit; in most cases this is associated with incorrect training of the horse, or ineffective riding. Since a severe bit requires particularly skilful and tactful use if the horse is to go better, rather than increasingly badly, such a bit is inappropriate in the hands of an ineffective rider.

It has to be admitted that there are some horses who may perform better in a different bit, an example being those who, out of boldness rather than anxiety, tend to really 'take on' their fences, including large solid uprights! With such horses, astute use of a potentially more severe bit may facilitate the necessary 'collecting' process on the approach, but it is crucially important that the horse respects the bit, rather than fears it. The rider who uses a bit which makes the horse afraid of going forward into the contact, or whose application of the bit has the same effect, has no chance of achieving good results, and is taking the first steps towards teaching the horse to nap and rear.

Should it prove really necessary to use a stronger bit (with positive results), it makes sense to keep that bit for important occasions, and to do all other riding in something milder. The benefits are two-fold:

1) Hopefully, continued riding and schooling in the milder bit may improve the horse's way of going, so that the more severe bit becomes unnecessary.

2) Using the more severe bit sparingly will help to retain the

horse's respect for it, thus avoiding any temptation for the rider to try something yet more severe, which is the first step on the road to disaster.

As far as other equipment is concerned, over-reach boots perform a useful protective function, especially in slippery conditions. Whereas the old-style boots required wrestling skills to fit and remove, there are now patterns available which can be simply strapped on, and there is little excuse for not fitting them.

Exercise bandages are, at best, a two-edged sword. It takes some skill to apply them correctly, and, if they are put on too tight, or knotted over a tendon, they can cause serious damage. Applied too loosely, they come unwound and flap around the horse's legs. They should not be necessary on a sound horse ridden with consideration, and should certainly not be applied for show, or in order to salve the conscience of a rider expecting a horse with suspect legs to perform on unsuitable ground. If they are used, there should be a protective layer of gamgee or similar material beneath them.

Consideration after Riding

We have already dealt with the basics of riding a tired horse home after hunting, and these, of course, apply after any other strenuous activity. If a horse is boxed to an event, there is the advantage of being able to take useful equipment with you, grooming kit, sweat-scraper, anti-sweat sheet and first-aid kit being fairly obvious items. It is also worth taking drinking water (and a bucket) for the horse, since this can be surprisingly difficult to obtain at many events. Although care must be taken as to when and how a horse is watered during an active day it is neither desirable nor necessary to deprive him of a drink altogether.

After having done concentrated fast work, the horse must be unsaddled and walked round in an anti-sweat rug until he is dry, and his respiration and pulse have returned to normal. He must not be left tied up and dripping with sweat while his rider disappears rapidly in the direction of the beer tent.

Once home, a tired horse will not appreciate over-much fussing about. You should do just enough to get him reasonably clean, dry and comfortable, and leave the fancy grooming until next day. After a hard day, it is usually appropriate to give a rather 'softer' feed than normal but, if the horse is to have his regular rations, these should be preceded by a small feed of hay, which will help relax him and stimulate his digestive system.

Conclusion

The pleasure of riding across country on a keen, fit, well-trained horse cannot easily be surpassed and, if this book helps to enhance the reader's enjoyment of his chosen sport, it will have fulfilled its purpose.

I hope, however, that the reader will realise that this enjoyment is, in part, dependent upon an acceptance of the rider's role in maintaining the horse in such condition. Those who seek to improve their riding should not, therefore, think merely of using the horse in pursuit of pleasure, but rather of trying to improve each horse they ride.